Southern Living GARDEN GUIDE

Annuals

Series Editor: Lois Trigg Chaplin

Oxmoor House.

Contents

©1996 by Oxmoor House, Inc.
Book Division of Southern Progress Corporation
P.O. Box 2463, Birmingham, Alabama 35201

Southern Living® is a federally registered
trademark of Southern Living, Inc.

Library of Congress Catalog Number: 95-74602
ISBN: 0-8487-2240-X
Manufactured in the United States of America
First Printing 1996

Editor-in-Chief: Nancy Fitzpatrick Wyatt
Editorial Director, Special Interest Publications:
Ann H. Harvey
Senior Editor, Editorial Services: Olivia Kindig Wells
Art Director: James Boone

Southern Living Garden Guide ANNUALS

Series Editor: Lois Trigg Chaplin
Assistant Editor: Kelly Hooper Troiano
Copy Editor: Jennifer K. Mathews
Editorial Assistant: Catherine Barnhart Pewitt
Garden Editor, *Southern Living*: Linda C. Askey
Indexer: Katharine R. Wiencke
Concept Designer: Eleanor Cameron
Designer: Carol Loria
Senior Photographer, *Southern Living*: Van Chaplin
Production and Distribution Director: Phillip Lee
Production Manager: Gail Morris
Associate Production and Distribution Manager:
John Charles Gardner
Associate Production Manager: Theresa L. Beste
Production Assistant: Marianne Jordan Wilson

Our appreciation to the staff of *Southern Living*
magazine for their contributions to this book.

Larkspur and hollyhocks

Lantana

Cover: *Morning glories*

Poppies

Annuals Primer

Paint a landscape for all seasons with annuals. They can be planted in great sweeps of vivid color or in single pots of one delicate hue.

Annuals, such as this spider flower, bloom, produce seed, and die within a year.

Pansies in a strawberry jar provide color in fall, winter, and early spring.

In the simplest of terms, an *annual* is a plant that sprouts, blooms, makes seed, and dies within a single year. But this in no way describes the versatility of these plants as they bring new color, new combinations, and new texture to a garden. The majority of annuals are planted in the spring, bloom through summer and fall, and are killed by frost. These are called *warm-weather annuals* and include such popular plants as impatiens, rose verbena, and globe amaranth. Other annuals are planted in fall or early spring and flower through the cool months. These are *cool-weather annuals*, such as poppies, pansies, and sweet peas, which bloom until high temperatures cause their decline.

A *perennial* is a plant that blooms year after year, such as an iris. A few plants that are perennial in the North are grown as cool-weather annuals in the South. Planted in the fall, they bloom in the spring and then die in summer's blazes. It is important to recognize how perennials are different from annuals.

Another group of plants you will find sold with annuals are *biennials.* You should know which plants are biennials, because these do not behave like annuals or perennials. Instead, biennials live for two years. In the first growing season, they produce plenty of foliage but no blooms; flowers appear the second year. Three popular biennials are foxglove, hollyhock, and sweet William. If you sow the seeds of these plants, do not expect them to bloom until the second year. However, the plants that you buy at a garden center will have probably spent some time in a greenhouse, so they will bloom the year you plant them as if they were annuals. Others are hybridized to bloom in their first season, although they are botanically biennial.

No matter which selections you choose, these pages will give you ideas and information for growing annuals to enjoy year-round.

Impatiens often self-sow, reappearing on their own from seed dropped the previous year.

ANNUALS THAT SEED THEMSELVES

Some annuals will drop seeds as they mature. Then, if the weather and soil in your garden are just right, you will see new plants reappear the next year. You may be fooled into thinking that they are perennials, but they are not. They are simply annuals that reestablish themselves from seed as nature intended. The offspring may be different heights and colors from the original, but such surprises are part of the fun of gardening.

Black-eyed Susan
Calliopsis
Cosmos
Four o'clock
Globe amaranth
Iceland poppy
Impatiens
Klondyke cosmos
Madagascar periwinkle
Marigold
Melampodium
Shirley poppy
Snow-on-the-mountain
Spider flower
Sunflower
Sweet pea
Zinnia

Annuals in the Landscape

You bring instant color to your garden with every annual that you plant. Unlike more permanent plants, annuals can provide a changing palette of colors from year to year.

Large masses of color, such as these yellow pansies, bring continuity to a flower bed.

Ideas for Placement

The more you work with annuals, the more you realize how forgiving they are. If you plant the wrong color, you can pick something new for the following year. Take advantage of this flexibility to try new things.

Here are some suggestions for placing annuals in your garden in relation to each other and to other types of plants. Also, study the photographs for suggestions they make. In gardening, doing is learning, but seeing is the next best thing.

Masses of Color in Large Beds

You can group annuals in a flower bed to create a sweep of solid color or to intermingle with other blocks of color. For large masses, think in terms of plant groups, using an entire flat or more of the same variety planted in gentle curves. This is most effective with pansies, Madagascar periwinkle, narrowleaf zinnias, and other plants that knit together to create a "carpet."

For the most striking show, beds should be a minimum of 3 feet wide, preferably wider, and as long as your back and budget will allow. Some beds may even extend the length of the property. When using groups of annuals as part of a tapestry of many colors, you should plant enough of the same plant, usually 3 to 10, to make a respectable group.

Spots of Color in the Garden

On the other hand, many annuals are bound to end up in small beds because there is a limit to your time, space, or money. In this case, remember to use the spots of color in places where you want people to look, for flowers will attract the eye. Do not plant annuals to "hide" the air-conditioning unit or other eyesore; flowers simply draw more attention to it. Use annuals to mark the entrance to your home, the foot of a fountain or a birdbath, a patio cutout, or any other carefully identified spaces. Spots of color call for an annual that looks good for the longest possible time, such as Madagascar periwinkle, impatiens, wax begonia, or melampodium.

Red geraniums lend spots of color to an evergreen entry.

Here and There as Filler

Annuals work well when used to fill in between perennials and shrubs in a bed. Because they bloom for months, their color is a constant you can count on as other plants fade. Annuals are also a nice tool for unifying a mixed planting. Try repeating one or two types throughout a bed to bring unity.

A window box practically brings flowers into the house. Remember to keep it watered, as it dries out quickly like any container. (Petunias, marigolds, artemisia, veronica, bacopa, asters, asparagus fern)

Pots Put Color Anywhere

Growing annuals in pots allows you to put the color right where you want it. Typical places include patios, decks, and window boxes, but you can even move pots indoors for a temporary decoration. The bright blooms bring instant color indoors, and containers also provide a simple way to maintain color outdoors at minimal expense.

Even if you have not planted a formal garden, you can plan a succession of potted flowers year-round. Pots are easier to reach and maintain than garden beds, and they require fewer tools. You may mix annuals in a large pot to provide a variety of color and form. Pair upright plants, such as geraniums or dusty miller, with cascading ones like petunias, sweet alyssum, or purslane.

Hanging baskets, another type of container, allow plants to dangle. You may use special stands to hold a collection of baskets, or you might hang baskets from eaves, arbors, upper porch rails—almost anywhere. However, the drawback to all containers is that they need water every day in hot weather.

Window boxes are a third type of container that bring your flowers into perfect view from indoors. Always popular for the front of the house, window boxes are ideal for the window of a child's room or that of a housebound person. A window box is a wonderful way to enjoy various annuals each season.

Annuals for a Cutting Garden

The ideal way to grow flowers for cutting is to not be concerned with clashing colors or plant heights. The most practical cutting garden has its own space set apart from the landscape and is planted in rows instead of in groups arranged by color and size. This format lets you replace plants as they wane without upsetting the layout and allows extra spacing between plants so that

A garden for cutting will provide sunflowers, zinnias, and dozens of other blooms to bring indoors.

the flowers can grow large and their stems strong. Plants crammed close together in a flower border are not the best flowers for cutting because crowding makes the stems thin and weak.

A Garden from Seed

One of today's most popular garden styles, the cottage garden, actually dates back to a time when landscaping and garden design were hardly priorities. The original cottage gardeners used plants they already had, were given, or could start from seed. Plants were not always placed according to strict design principles; many plants were left alone to grow where they seeded themselves.

You can achieve a cottage garden flower bed by starting flowers from seed. Starting from seed is less expensive than buying transplants, but it requires more patience as you nurture seedlings and control weeds. Turn to page 22 for more on the specifics of seed sowing.

This garden of zinnias and spider flower was started from seed in early summer and reached full bloom within 10 weeks.

PRACTICAL POINTERS

• Put the tallest plants toward the back of a bed that has a wall or structure behind it, or plant them in the center of a bed that will be viewed from all sides.

• Remember plant compatibility. What makes your plants grow best: sun or shade, wet or dry soil? Do not mix plants with opposite needs or your bed will have a ragged appearance as one plant thrives and another one struggles.

• When mixing annuals with other plants, do not plant just one unless it is very large, such as a tall, bushy coleus or lantana. Instead, plant in trios. Place three plants in the ground so that they form a triangle. They will grow together to make one clump, which will have more visual impact than a single plant.

• When planning a large flower bed, remember that it will look more lush and full if you design it to be viewed down its length.

Colors and Combinations

You will enjoy your garden most when you use flowers and foliage to paint a picture that changes with the seasons. Translating a rainbow of flowers into an orchestrated design calls for a careful study of the annuals available to you. Look into color and texture combinations as if you were decorating a room. In short, a little planning helps when planting a flower garden.

Start with the Color Wheel

While selecting color is a matter of personal taste, the color wheel on this page shows how colors naturally work together. The wheel is an artist's tool for previewing the impact of certain color combinations and helps simplify color selection. To use this color wheel, cut a small equilateral triangle of paper and position it on the wheel so that its points are on the three primary colors—red, yellow, and blue. As you rotate the triangle, the points show trios of complementary colors that work well together, making it easy for you to group flowers of corresponding colors.

Also consider the color of your home and the surrounding areas when planning your garden. For instance, red brick does not make a good backdrop for red flowers, but red blooms are exquisite against a gray wall or sidewalk.

Using Color in the Garden

• *Start with green.* For a successful foreground of flowers, you need a background of green. Evergreen shrubs are especially nice during the winter months because they provide constant foliage if the bed is otherwise dormant.

Evergreen trees and shrubs provide a rich background for flowers. Here snapdragons do indeed snap against the dark evergreens.

Pots filled with wax begonias add spots of color to this terrace.

• **Punctuate with color.** The use of color for bold accents is limited only by your imagination. Consider a spot of strong color near an entryway to define it and attract attention; if you have a primarily evergreen garden, use color in pots or beds to enliven the green.

• **Use colors to impart mood.** Warm colors—red, orange, and bright yellow—attract attention by suggesting both sunshine and flame. They make a garden happy and lively, and can also make it warm and cozy.

Such colors become good choices for the winter and early spring garden but are perhaps less appealing for summer, when you do not need to add warmth. In contrast, white, blue, and pastel flowers seem cooler and are pleasant choices for a tree-shaded spot in the summertime.

Petunias, annual phlox, and verbena in shades of purple, red, and deep pink combine with yellow sedum to give this bed a warm glow in early spring.

Pale colors of impatiens, geraniums, and petunias were carefully chosen for this courtyard to help create a sense of spaciousness and distance.

• *Use color to control space.* Warm-colored blooms attract your eye and stand out against the background. They are more noticeable, tending to come forward in the landscape, thereby shrinking the space between the plant and your eye. Warm-colored blooms can make a large garden feel smaller and more intimate. On the other hand, the cool colors—especially blue and violet—tend to recede, so cool-colored blooms are minimized and make a small space seem larger.

• *Use color to unify.* Repeating one shade of blooms, such as white, will bring unity to an assortment of colored flowers.

• *Use white for nighttime enjoyment.* White is both striking and clearly visible under moonlight or outdoor lighting. The most effective white flowers are flat blooms, such as those of moonflower and impatiens. Light-colored foliage, like the big leaves of white caladiums, also shows up well after dark. Because nighttime is often the

White blooms, such as this large, flat moonflower, show up well in moonlight and night lighting.

only opportunity you have to enjoy a deck or patio, always consider white flowers for at least one spot in your garden.

• *Use blue liberally for various effects.* You can create excitement by pairing color-wheel opposites, such as blue with orange or yellow. For a quieter mood, combine blue with white, silver, or violet; these shades emphasize the coolness of blue.

Annuals with Attractive Foliage

Some annuals, such as silver-leafed dusty miller, are more prized for their foliage than for their flowers. Others, such as coleus, are grown solely for the colors of their leaves. These annuals can lift a bed from ordinary to extraordinary by giving the viewer a surprise. Just when you expect flowers, leaves instead create the show. Chartreuse coleus foliage contrasts vividly with deep-colored flowers, and the dark maroon type is a perfect foil for pinks in both vivid and pale shades.

The silver foliage of dusty miller is every bit as showy as a flower, if not more so. The fuzzy, silvery-white leaves beckon from a distance and shimmer in both sunlight and moonlight. You can use silver to enhance any color, as it provides a gentle backdrop to the richness of purple globe amaranth, orange marigolds, and other annuals pale or bright. Place silvery foliage behind a green-leafed plant, such as the fan-shaped bearded iris, to create a stunning silhouette. Like white flowers, silver foliage is more prominent than green at night.

Finally, consider a variegated annual, such as snow-on-the-mountain; such foliage becomes an accent when surrounded by darker leaves and enlivens any nearby flowers with its contrasting colors. Joseph's coat is another popular variegated annual that you can keep trimmed as a boxlike edging for a formal herb bed or parterre garden.

Chartreuse coleus is just one annual with unusually colored leaves that are as showy as a flower.

The silver leaves of dusty miller bring out the best of other colors.

A Few Good Combinations

Cool and Quiet
Bachelor's button and pale pink sweet William
Blue pansy and white sweet alyssum
Dusty miller and blue ageratum
Pale pink sweet William and white pansy

Warm and Vibrant
Blue pansy and yellow pansy
Blue pansy and red tulip
Dark pink snapdragon and deep yellow pansy
Hot pink petunia and orange marigold
Scarlet sage and Mexican mint marigold

Plantings for Each Season

Planning around the seasons is the key to keeping yearlong color in your garden. The photos on these pages show some colorful examples of seasonal annuals. The reward comes in mixing annuals that overlap the seasons with perennials and shrubs that may bloom for only a short time. Annuals provide long-lasting sweeps of vivid color that you may change from year to year.

Summer: Caladiums, mealycup sage, coleus, and white impatiens provide months of color on this terrace from spring until frost strikes in the fall.

Fall: Narrowleaf zinnia, white impatiens, and mealycup sage linger from summer into fall to mix with the autumn tones of perennial sedum as it comes into bloom.

A GARDEN JOURNAL

Annuals in a landscape need to be replaced at the end of the season, lest you have a bed of dying plants. Keep a journal or notebook to jot down selections of plants that pleased you so that you will be sure to buy them again. Record those that did not work well to avoid future disappointment. Your notebook may be as detailed as you wish. Entries could include planting dates, disease or insect problems and solutions, length of bloom, cold hardiness, tolerance to rainy weather, and anything else that will help you next time around.

Getting Started

Starting with healthy plants and reliable information about planting and caring for your annuals will be the key to their success.

Transplants come in many sizes. Large plants have an immediate impact, but younger transplants catch up to them quickly. (Madagascar periwinkle, marigolds, globe amaranth, narrowleaf zinnia)

Consumer Horticulture

When you shop for groceries, you generally enter the supermarket with a good idea of what you need to buy. When you visit the garden center, you should know how many plants you will need to start a bed, and whether you want to start with transplants or from seed.

About Transplants

Transplants are seedlings that have been grown in small pots to be planted late in the garden. They give you a head start over seeding directly in the garden. Often many of the varieties sold as transplants are difficult to start from seed at home. The most economical way to purchase transplants is in flats that hold *cell packs,* small plastic "four-packs" or "six-packs" of plants. Smaller plants are ideal for planting early in the season when there is adequate time for them to grow. However, most annuals grow very fast, often reaching their mature size within 8 to 12 weeks after planting.

Here are a few tips to help you with the practical questions that will arise when buying flats of bedding plants. Most flats hold 24 to 48 plants, depending on the size of the packs. Packs may have three, four, or six cells each. Always water a flat thoroughly before removing the transplants for planting. If transplants are even slightly dry, they may be difficult to properly water once planted.

You will also find flats that contain plants grown in 4-inch pots. Four-inch pots come 16 to a flat, with one plant per pot. The larger size of these plants is an advantage, especially if you plant them late in the growing season. As the year progresses, nurseries sometimes sell large, mature annuals in 8-inch and gallon-sized containers. These can be planted for instant color. However, if planted late in the season, transplants require very diligent watering to make a good transition to pot or ground.

How To Select Transplants

If you have a choice between small and large plants, always choose the small ones. It is best to buy transplants that have not yet started blooming. Older plants in small cells often have become rootbound, with their roots growing through the bottom of the cell or tightly wound within. Ideally, you want to plant a young, green plant and give it a chance to develop plenty of new foliage before it begins to bloom. Although purchasing transplants before they bloom does not allow you to see the color of the flowers, these younger plants will transplant with the least shock; those that are large and rootbound will need extra care.

Check that each cell in the flat contains a healthy plant. If foliage appears mottled, look at the underside of the leaves for aphids, whiteflies, or spider mites. If the transplants appear weak, slip one out of the pack to check the roots. Healthy roots are white and fibrous; soft or brown roots are a sign of disease.

It is also crucial that you purchase transplants that have been properly cared for. Those that spend days baking in a sidewalk display and are allowed to severely wilt between waterings will not grow into healthy plants.

PLANT PURCHASING GUIDE

Spacing Between Plants	Plants per Square Foot
6 inches	4.41
8	2.60
10	1.66
12	1.15
15	0.738
18	0.512
24	0.290

BUYING FOR MASS PLANTING

When planning a large bed, it is important to determine the number of transplants you will need. You want to purchase enough the first time because your supplier may not be able to restock immediately if he runs out of a particular plant.

Use the Plant Purchasing Guide on this page to determine how many plants you will need per square foot of garden. Read the label to find the recommended spacing for your plant. Multiply the number of plants needed per square foot by the number of square feet in your bed. This will be the total number of plants you will need.

Example: A bed 6 feet deep and 10 feet wide has 60 square feet of planting area. If the label recommends spacing the plants 8 inches apart, then multiply 2.6 times 60 for a total of 156 plants to fill the bed.

Sunflowers grow from seed to their full height in one season.

EASY TO START FROM SEED

Calliopsis

Cosmos

Globe amaranth

Klondyke cosmos

Marigold

Morning glory

Spider flower

Sunflower

Sweet pea

Zinnia

How To Buy Seed

Some plants, such as cosmos and spider flower, are rarely found as transplants because they grow unwieldy very quickly. To grow them, you must purchase seed from either a garden center or a mail-order seed company and start your own transplants, or sow seed directly in the garden. Just remember that starting from seed is more economical than buying transplants only if you do it right.

Always buy seed dated for the current year, and only purchase packets that have been properly stored in a cool, dry environment. Seed in packets that are wrinkled with moisture or left sitting in the sun may have lost their viability.

Flowers whose seeds germinate quickly are easy to start directly in the garden.

Storing Transplants and Seed

When you cannot plant everything the day you bring it home, make sure you keep the plants and seed in top condition until you can get them in the ground. Place transplants outdoors in partial shade, with protection from afternoon sun, and water daily. If they sit for more than two weeks, water with a diluted liquid fertilizer, such as fish emulsion or commercial houseplant fertilizer. Try not to wait more than a week or two or the plants will quickly become rootbound and stunted.

Store unused seed in a sealed plastic container in the refrigerator or freezer. Never leave them in an outdoor storage room or anywhere they might be exposed to water or humidity.

Breaking Ground

The annuals you plant are only as good as the conditions you provide for them. Granted, some annuals tolerate neglect better than others, but all do best with some basic care. If you give them the right amount of sunlight, good soil, and proper watering and feeding, they will grow larger and bear more flowers than poorly tended plants.

Preparing the Planting Bed

The ideal soil is loose enough to allow roots to easily expand and is porous, well drained, and able to retain moisture and nutrients. But such soil is rarely found naturally around your home. You must create your own by adding wheelbarrow loads of organic matter, such as compost, manure, or sphagnum peat moss. Organic matter improves clay soil by opening it up so that roots can properly breathe and drain. On the other hand, it helps poor, sandy soil hold more moisture and nutrients.

Good soil preparation is a key to success in the garden.

HINTS FOR BREAKING NEW GROUND

• When testing your soil, take samples from different parts of the area to get an accurate reading.

• Mark the outline of a new bed by stretching a garden hose out in the shape of the bed, or draw the proposed edges with spray paint. The lines will help you keep your grass-and-weed killer within bounds.

• Never work the soil when it is wet, as it will dry in clods. However, tilling is easier if the soil is slightly moist, especially heavy clay soil. Water the day before tilling, or plan your project to follow a light rain.

A garden hose makes easy work of defining the outline of a new flower bed. To kill grass and weeds within the outline, spray with a nonselective herbicide a week or two before turning the soil.

19

Compost provides organic matter to help keep the soil workable.

BE PREPARED

To make each replanting a little easier, keep a layer of mulch on top of the bed, even if it lies unplanted for a season. This will help prevent the growth of weeds and will continue to add organic matter to the soil as the mulch decomposes.

When possible, begin preparing your soil a couple of weeks before planting so that you can do the job in stages rather than all at once. If the spot has never been cultivated, begin by removing anything growing there. You can transplant healthy grass to bare spots elsewhere in the yard or spray the entire area with a nonselective herbicide to kill existing grass and weeds. Remember that these products will kill everything green that they touch, so follow label directions carefully. Once in the ground, these substances decompose to nitrogen, water, phosphate, and carbon dioxide. In a week to 10 days you can break up the dead vegetation with a turning fork or tiller and remove it to a compost pile.

Use a turning fork to work the soil as deeply as possible, preferably 12 to 18 inches in heavy clay. Rent a tiller for large beds. Never work wet soil as it will dry in clods. Spread a layer of organic matter 3 to 4 inches deep over the area and work this with your fork until well blended with the native soil.

Each time you work organic matter into the soil it becomes softer, making your work easier. The first time is always the most difficult.

Always Do a Soil Test

You may have trouble assessing your soil's chemistry. Is the soil acidity (pH) too high or low? How much nitrogen, phosphorus, and potassium does it need? In certain areas of the country, salt levels are high; in others, the native soil may be deficient of a crucial element. A soil test will tell you what your soil needs.

Soil test kits are available through your county Agricultural Extension service office. The kit contains directions for testing, along with a form to record your findings. Most states charge a small fee, but it is well worth the cost to determine exactly what your soil needs to yield beautiful, healthy plants.

Collect soil samples to be analyzed for soil pH and serious deficiencies or excesses of plant nutrients in your soil.

Planting

Proper planting is essential to the success of your annuals. Their health and vigor will be best if they get a good start, which includes everything from the way you handle the plants to the soil in which they grow.

Handling Transplants

When you bring transplants home, keep them watered and in partial sun until you are ready to plant. Ideally, you should plant right away; try to plant them within one week.

Remove a transplant from its pot by turning the pot upside down and sliding the plant out. Never grab the stem and pull it or you may tear it from its roots. Remember, young plants need to be handled gently.

Sometimes you have no choice but to purchase plants that are a bit rootbound. This is common with ageratum, marigolds, pansies, and globe amaranth. In this case, you may gently score the roots with a sharp knife, making one vertical cut just through the surface on each side of the root ball. If the roots are big enough, such as in a hanging basket or gallon pot, gently pull a few away from the tangled mass. These procedures will help the roots grow out of their tangle and into their new bed. Otherwise, the tangled roots will stay exactly the size they were when planted and the plant will not grow.

Perhaps the step you will find most difficult is the last one: remove the flowers from your young transplants when you plant them. They need to grow larger before beginning to produce flowers, so the bigger and leafier the plant, the more it will bloom. Simply pinch off large flowers, such as marigolds, or snip smaller blooms, such as sweet alyssum, with scissors. To help keep the plants active, fertilize with a liquid plant food, such as 20-20-20, immediately after planting.

Overgrown, rootbound transplants, such as these marigolds, need their roots untangled so that they will grow into the flower bed. Snipping off blooms also helps plants grow larger before blooming again.

Setting Transplants in the Bed

Always set a transplant at the same depth it was planted in its original container. The top of the root ball should be level with the surface of the soil. Pat the soil around the plants firmly, but do not pack it down. The idea is to eliminate air pockets and be sure the root ball is in firm contact with the soil.

Press transplants firmly into the soil.

Space transplants according to the directions on the label. Although spacing is never exact and will vary among selections of the same plant, remember that plants placed too close together will compete for space. This will cause their stems to weaken as they stretch for light and soil. Second to your experience, the plant label will provide you with the most accurate spacing information because it is selection specific. (Note: Do not buy plants that are not labeled. Plants have traits specific to each selection, which will affect their successful placement.)

If you are planting a large bed, place plants in a staggered grid pattern as illustrated, rather than in even rows. This pattern ensures proper spacing and gives the bed a more organized look.

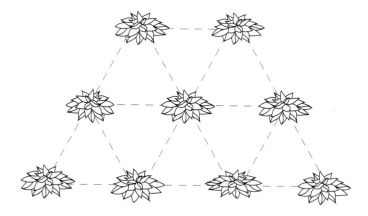

Planting in a diamond-grid pattern gives a more uniform look to a new planting.

Seeding Directly in the Garden

Sowing seeds directly in the garden has several advantages: it involves less work than starting your own transplants, it costs less, and the seedlings do not suffer transplant shock.

To prepare the soil for seeding, loosen with a turning fork or a tiller just as you would to set out transplants. There should be plenty of organic matter worked into the bed. It is also crucial that you rake the ground level and smooth so that the seeds will stay in place. Poke large seeds, such as sunflower seeds, gently into the ground at half the recommended spacing.

Loose, rich soil allows seedlings to break through the surface easily.

After the seedlings are 2 to 3 inches high, you can thin to the recommended spacing so that they are not too crowded. Plant at the recommended depth or slightly more shallow. It is better to plant a bit shallow than too deep, as seeds buried too deep will not germinate.

Try to scatter seeds so that they fall about three times closer than the spacing recommended on the package. Smaller seeds should be spread over the entire bed and then pressed firmly into the soil. Do not try to bury them—instead, press them into the soil with the back of your hand, fingers together, or walk on a piece of plywood placed over the seeded area.

Water Is Essential

The key to raising seedlings is water. *Never* let the soil dry out. Use a mister or a fine sprinkler nozzle on your garden hose to keep the area moist. Water once a day until the seedlings are 1 to 2 inches tall; then water frequently enough to keep the soil moist but not soggy.

Thin the Seedlings

Finally, be sure to thin the seedlings as soon as the first true leaves appear. The first two leaves that poke through the ground are not true leaves but rather **cotyledons,** or seedling leaves, which provide energy. The next pair to appear are the true leaves, the first leaves that are shaped like those of a mature plant, only smaller, and are usually visible within a week after sprouting. Thin seedlings to half the recommended spacing at first, and then thin again a week or two later to the spacing recommended on the seed packet.

You can raise the level of the soil to improve drainage by building a bed on top of the ground. Till the native soil as if preparing it for planting. This helps the soil in the raised area drain into the ground below.

There are endless ways to build a raised bed, ranging from simply mounding the soil about a foot high to building a box from landscape timbers, mortared brick, or stacked stone. When filling the raised bed, be sure to incorporate native soil along with compost or a soil mix. (Do not include native soil if you have had problems with plants rotting at the base or roots, or if plants have been stunted by nematodes.)

A raised bed will improve drainage on low ground.

Starting Transplants Indoors

One of the advantages to growing your own transplants is that you can grow selections that are not locally available. Sometimes this is the only way to have the plants that you want. Growing transplants from seed also allows you to time your plantings just when you want them, without relying upon availability at the garden center. This is especially nice for fall-planted annuals, such as poppies.

Seed-Starting Tips

• The seeds of most flowers will germinate at a soil temperature of 65 to 70 degrees. This temperature is easy to achieve indoors, away from cold drafts and windows. You may place the seeded flat on top of the refrigerator or water heater until the seeds sprout.

• Do not be tempted to use garden soil for starting seeds, as it may contain diseases. Soil mixes for starting seeds are both sterile and lightweight, which allows easy germination, and contain a starter fertilizer to boost growth.

• Allow six weeks for seedlings to germinate. Time your seed sowing by counting back six weeks from the earliest date you can transplant. After that time, you can move them outdoors where they will both strengthen and grow more quickly.

• Fertilize weekly with a half-strength solution of liquid fertilizer, such as 20-20-20, before transplanting. Ideally, plants should be 3 to 4 inches tall with sturdy stems and well-formed roots when transplanted.

Be sure to place seedlings in a sunny window or under a plant light so that they will develop properly. Without enough light they will be weak and spindly.

- Seedlings need cool nighttime temperatures (60 to 65 degrees); high nighttime temperatures may cause spindly growth.

- Save used cell packs. Use them to start your own seeds indoors. Sterilize used packs with a weak solution of one part bleach to nine parts water.

- Place young seedlings in dappled shade before planting. Seedlings transplanted directly from your house to the garden will be shocked.

A Step-by-Step Method

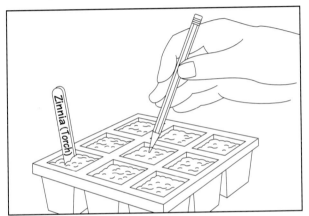

Sow seeds directly in a sterile container filled with a soil mix specially formulated for starting seeds. Be sure to water the flat before sowing. For fine seeds, use tweezers or the moistened tip of a pencil to place seeds in the containers; do not bury the seeds, but press them firmly into the mix.

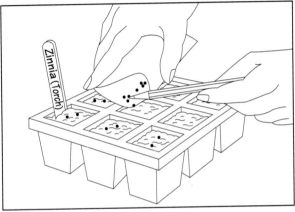

Sow two seeds in each cell for insurance. (Snip one off at the soil level with nail scissors if both seeds sprout.) Be sure to label each pack with the name and selection of the plant and the planting date. Flat wooden sticks and a fine-tip permanent marker work well.

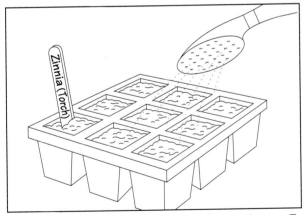

Keep the flat watered with the fine spray of a watering can. To conserve moisture, place the flat in a clear plastic bag, but remove it when the seedlings appear. Do not use a bag if you place the flat on a warm surface, such as a water heater.

In all likelihood, more than one seed will germinate. When this occurs, snip off the smaller seedling.

Caring for Annuals

Globe amaranth

The final step for the success of your annuals is caring for them after they are planted. Whether in the ground or in a pot, annuals need water and food to supply energy and mulch to keep the roots cool and moist. They will reward you with months of glorious color when cared for properly.

Care in the Garden

Once you have prepared the soil and gotten your plants in the ground, taking care of your outdoor annuals requires little effort. Water, fertilizer, and a bit of individual attention make the difference between a flower bed that sits idle and one that grows full of blooms. Maintaining your garden is easy if you follow these steps from the very beginning.

Watering

Annuals need more frequent watering when first planted. Later on, established plants require less water, especially the more hardy species. Many methods of watering will work: use a sprinkler or a soaker hose, or simply hold your garden hose over the plants. The key is to water thoroughly to encourage deep rooting. Shallow watering will keep roots close to the surface, making plants more susceptible to drought.

How much water is enough? Generally, an inch of water per application gets water deep enough in most soil types. You can measure an inch by placing several soup cans or inexpensive rain gauges in the range of your sprinkler (place pans under soaker hoses). When the containers have collected an inch of water, you will know how long it takes to deliver a proper application.

ANNUALS THAT ARE VERY TOLERANT OF DROUGHT

These flowers bounce back if they go a week or more without watering, even during hot, dry weather.

Black-eyed Susan
Globe amaranth
Klondyke cosmos
Madagascar periwinkle
Moss rose
Purslane
Spider flower

Do not apply an inch of water all at once if your bed is sloped or the soil drains poorly. Instead, apply until the water puddles or runs off, turn the sprinkler off for an hour or so to let the water soak in, and then reapply. Remember that sandy soils do not hold water well and will dry out faster than clay or rich organic soil.

You do not have to stand watch or come home early just to turn off your sprinkler. If you do not have an automatic irrigation system, you can install an inexpensive timer at the spigot. Models range from mechanical types that simply turn off the water after a set number of minutes (like a kitchen timer) to computerized types that program several days at a time (ideal when you are away on vacation).

Another way to make watering easier is to lay a soaker hose in the bed before setting out your transplants. Made of a porous material, a soaker hose allows water to seep out along its length. If the bed is longer than 20 feet, choose a hose less than $\frac{5}{8}$ inch in diameter to ensure better pressure and thus a better flow of water along the length of the soaker hose. Use snap-type couplers to make quick work of hooking and unhooking your garden hose to the soaker.

Mulching

Mulch covers the ground like a blanket to help deter the growth of weeds and keep the soil moist. Organic mulches, such as bark, compost, and shredded leaves, build the richness of your soil as they decompose. Choose your mulch based on the terrain of your garden. Pine straw clings to gentle slopes better than other mulches because the needles knit together.

Apply the mulch 2 to 4 inches thick. The easiest way to mulch with pine straw is to apply the mulch *before* planting. After the soil is worked and raked smooth for planting, spread the mulch over the area. As you set transplants, push a bit of the pine straw aside to clear a spot for each plant; this is easier than trying to knit the long needles together around and between plants after they are in the ground. If you use bark, compost, or other material that is easily spread, set transplants first and spread the mulch by hand or shovel between the plants. When transplants are small, you can cover each with a plastic cup and work quickly without fear of burying a plant. Simply lift the cups when the bed is mulched.

Shredded leaves are an excellent mulch and soil conditioner.

Fertilizing

One look at the fertilizer shelf at the local garden center just might make you want to turn and run. With so many brands and formulas to choose from, you may feel a degree in chemistry would come in handy. However, if you arm yourself with a knowledge of what your plants need, you can feed your garden with minimal fuss.

The purpose of fertilization is to meet a plant's nutritional needs; these vary with both the age of the plant and the species. For example, a young transplant or seedling generally needs nitrogen early in its life to support rapid growth. Later, as the plant reaches its full size, nitrogen is less important, and you can encourage blooms with a fertilizer high in phosphorus and potassium but lower in nitrogen. A few plants, such as sweet peas, generally do not need fertilizer at all, because they can generate their own nitrogen provided a certain bacteria is present in the soil. In general, today's hybrid plants depend upon good fertilization to reach their full potential. Refer to the individual Plant Profile (beginning on page 35) to determine the fertilizer needs of a specific annual.

The easiest and most sensible approach to fertilization is to add adequate nutrients to the soil *before* you plant. In most cases, a good-quality, slow-release fertilizer will suffice. If you have performed a soil test, you are aware of any deficiencies or excesses that need correcting. In such cases, test results give specific recommendations to solve the problem.

To enrich your soil, you should always add compost or other organic matter that is rich in the many nutrients a plant needs. Then work a slow-release fertilizer into the soil before planting to ensure a constant supply of essential elements. If you use a chemical fertilizer, be sure to purchase one that contains at least half of its nitrogen in a slow-release form.

Organic gardeners may achieve similar results with slow-release organic fertilizers, such as blood meal or organic flower food, which depend upon soil bacteria to release their nitrogen as they decompose. These fertilizers yield good results and may increase microbial activity. Generally, organic fertilizers contain less nitrogen than their chemical counterparts. For example, blood meal is one of

A good slow-release fertilizer will feed your plants gradually so they will grow to their optimum size.

the highest in nitrogen, as it contains between 10 and 12 percent. Cottonseed meal contains about 6 perent nitrogen while composted chicken manure contains only 4 percent. If you compare cost per pound and quantity of nitrogen, these tend to be more expensive than chemical fertilizers.

To give young plants a boost, water them with a diluted fertilizer solution the first week or two after planting. Plants absorb this liquid food immediately. You may use an all-purpose mix, such as 20-20-20 or fish emulsion, on transplants.

The Fertilizer Label

By law, all fertilizers must carry a label stating the percentage of nutrients they contain. The three numbers always represent the percentage of nitrogen (N), phosphorus (P), and potassium (K). If the package is labelled 10-5-8, it contains 10 percent nitrogen, 5 percent phosphorus, and 8 percent potassium. These are the nutrients most required by a plant, so the combination of nitrogen, phosphorus, and potassium makes up what is called a *complete fertilizer.*

Nitrogen stimulates new growth, especially early foliage, which is why you need a good supply early in the growth cycle. Because nitrogen is very soluble and mobile in the soil, buy a product that contains a slow-release form. Otherwise, your nitrogen may be washed away before being absorbed.

Phosphorus encourages flowering and is essential for overall plant health. Bloom-boosting fertilizers contain a high percentage of phosphorus. However, too much phosphorus in the soil blocks a plant's ability to absorb other nutrients. Unless you are gardening in containers or your soil test indicates a deficiency, use a fertilizer low in phosphorus. Many suburban soils may be high in phosphorus if the land was once agricultural.

Potassium, also called potash on fertilizer labels, is essential to plant metabolism. It is crucial to a plant's cell wall structure as well as its ability to manufacture food. However, be sure to not use potassium in excess as it may burn your plants.

What Is a Slow-Release Fertilizer?

Slow-release fertilizer is sometimes called *controlled-release* because it releases small amounts of nutrients at a time. The nutrients are coated and held in reserve to be released gradually over several weeks or months, depending on soil moisture and temperature. This type of fertilizer is ideal for the busy gardener because it does not have to be applied often.

The label will indicate whether the fertilizer contains slow-release nitrogen. There is a wide price range depending on the percentage of coated nutrients a fertilizer contains. Look for one that contains at least 50 percent slow-release nitrogen.

Care of Annuals in Containers

Potted plants depend on you for soil, fertilizer, and water. Because their roots grow within the confines of a pot, they need more care than plants in the ground, but the color they bring to patios and windows is worth the extra effort.

Selecting Soil

Good soil is crucial to plants in containers. It must drain well and be free of soil-borne diseases or insects. Buy a premium-quality, sterile potting soil rather than using soil from the yard to fill your pot. *Potting soil,* a packaged soil mix made especially for growing plants in pots, is blended with composted bark, sphagnum peat moss, sand, perlite, or vermiculite. Some even contain starter fertilizer. Look for a potting soil that lists these quality ingredients.

Manufacturers of potting soil and bagged topsoil are not required to state the contents of their soil mix, so you will find a big difference in quality among brands. A poor soil can be too acid or too alkaline, may be prone to compaction, or may contain certain ingredients that are toxic to the plants. Price is generally a good indicator of quality. Do not be tempted to use leftover seed-starting mix for potting plants; such a mix is so lightweight that it does not provide a good anchor for large plants.

Set transplants in a pot at half the spacing recommended for the garden.

Fill pots to within an inch of the rim with a premium potting soil.

Planting in Containers

To plant in a container, cover the drainage hole with a piece of window screen or fine mesh. This lets excess water drain and keeps soil from leaking out. Fill the pot with sterile potting soil to within an inch of the rim (if too full, the soil will wash out when you water). Space transplants at half the spacing that you would use if planting them in the garden. If you start from seed, sow at the depth recommended on the packet and when the seedlings emerge, thin to about half the recommended spacing.

The organic matter in potting soil will decompose with time, so plan to refill your pots with fresh soil every other year. In warm, humid climates where decomposition occurs very quickly, such as Florida, you will need fresh soil every year. Recycle old soil by mixing it into your flower beds or compost pile.

A POTTING SOIL RECIPE

If you have several pots to fill, it is cheaper to mix your own potting soil. Here is a recipe for a good general mix.

Use a 3-gallon bucket to fill a 3-cubic-foot wheelbarrow with:

1 bucket sphagnum peat moss
1 bucket coarse sand
1 bucket finely ground bark
2 cups lime
$\frac{1}{3}$ pound iron sulfate
2 pounds slow-release flower food or 6 pounds cottonseed meal

Use your shovel to blend the ingredients. Stir well to be sure the soil is evenly mixed. Gently dampen the mix with a sprinkler, stopping every few minutes to turn the soil thoroughly. When the mix is moist (not soggy), it is ready to use. Store any leftover soil in a large plastic garbage can with a sealed lid.

Watering

Plants in containers dry out more quickly than those in the garden because their small volume of soil does not hold much water and their exposure to air and heat through the pot causes rapid evaporation. To make watering convenient, keep a hose and watering can nearby. Afternoon shade also reduces heat and stress on plants in midsummer.

Marigolds

In winter, it is easy to forget waterings because plants do not wilt as readily. However, if pansies or other winter annuals are dry when an Arctic blast comes along, they are much more likely to be damaged by the cold. You may also spray them with an ***antidesiccant*** (an agent that prevents visible wilting) to keep their foliage from drying, but do not forget to water.

Fertilizing

Unless a potting soil specifically states that it contains fertilizer, it is probably very low in the elements plants need for growth. Incorporate a slow-release fertilizer that also contains micronutrients into the mix when planting. Plants require frequent watering during the heat of the summer, which often cuts the life of the fertilizer by one-third to one-half. Be prepared to reapply during the growing season.

When filling pots, be sure to include a quality slow-release fertilizer to provide the nutrients the plants will need for growth.

Petunias and rose verbena are two of an endless number of combinations that will thrive in containers.

ANNUALS THAT THRIVE IN CONTAINERS

Although you can grow just about anything in a container if you give it enough care, the ideal plants require minimal maintenance. They are forgiving (should you forget to water) and stay low enough not to flop over or require staking. The following annuals do very well in pots and window boxes. Those marked with an asterisk (*) have stems long enough for hanging baskets or to spill over the edge of a planter.

Ageratum
Dusty miller
Geranium
Globe amaranth (dwarf types)
Johnny-jump-up
Lisianthus (dwarf types)
Madagascar periwinkle*
Marigold
Melampodium
Moss rose*
Narrowleaf zinnia*
Ornamental cabbage and kale
Pansy
Petunia
Purslane*
Rose verbena*
Sweet alyssum*
Trailing lantana*
Wax begonia

Plant Hardiness Zone Map

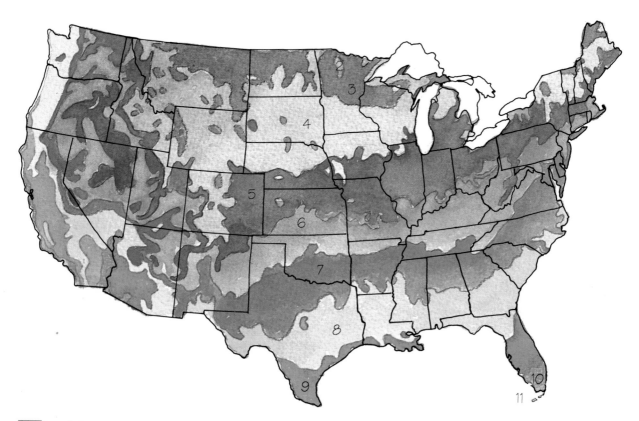

The United States Department of Agriculture has charted low temperatures throughout the country to determine the ranges of average low readings. The map above is based loosely on the USDA Plant Hardiness Zone Map, which was drawn from these findings. It does not take into account heat, soil, or moisture extremes and is intended as a guide, not a guarantee.

The southern regions of the United States that are mentioned in this book refer to the following:

Upper South: Zone 6

Middle South: upper region of Zone 7 (0 to 5 degrees minimum)

Lower South: lower region of Zone 7 and upper region of Zone 8 (5 to 15 degrees minimum)

Coastal South: lower region of Zone 8 and upper region of Zone 9 (15 to 25 degrees minimum)

Tropical South: lower region of Zone 9 and all of Zone 10 (25 to 40 degrees minimum)

Zone 2	-50	to	-40°F
Zone 3	-40	to	-30°F
Zone 4	-30	to	-20°F
Zone 5	-20	to	-10°F
Zone 6	-10	to	0°F
Zone 7	0	to	10°F
Zone 8	10	to	20°F
Zone 9	20	to	30°F
Zone 10	30	to	40°F
Zone 11		above	40°F

Plant Profiles

The annuals described in the following pages were selected by the garden editors at *Southern Living* on the basis of their beauty, adaptability, and value in the garden. They span the entire spectrum of annuals, from those that thrive anywhere—in full sun and sandy soil—to those that need rich soil and regular attention. Many are tried-and-true favorites that have worked for gardeners for years.

Arranged alphabetically by common name, these profiles give you a description of each plant, information about planting and care, and suggested ways that you can incorporate its color, height, and form into your garden. Critical to your success is knowing the soil and cultural conditions each plant needs; this information is contained in the profiles, as well as troubleshooting tips and solutions.

When a genus contains more than one related species, such as morning glory and moonflower, they are combined as a single entry. However, the description points out the differences in appearance and growing needs of the most popular species.

For a quick overview of the plant, refer to the *At a Glance* box that accompanies every profile. This will give you the major features of the annual, including its botanical name to help you avoid confusion when buying plants.

Try experimenting with new annuals in your garden each year. Feel free to plant those that you have never grown before or that are only marginally suited to your climate. You may find that even the most unexpected selections will flourish with your tender care; if not, you can begin again with a clean slate next year!

Zinnias

Caladiums

Ageratum

The fine-petaled flowers are borne in clusters.

It is so rare to find a flower that has blue blooms that gardeners feel they have a treasure in ageratum. Although ageratum comes in an assortment of hues, blue ageratum is prized for its unusual color. Ageratum is also one of the garden's longest lasting blues.

The clusters of ageratum create a dense blanket of flowers that is excellent for edging, planting in masses, or adding a bit of strong color to containers. The dwarf types stay compact, never sprawling or straying, and thus are well suited for a design that requires perfect edges or uniform height.

This plant was very popular during the Victorian era, when carpet bedding (large garden designs made with flowers) was popular. The same use applies today for parterre gardens, or for elaborate garden clocks and other designs painted with flowers across the landscape. Dwarf ageratum also does well in strawberry jars because the compact plants do not outgrow the "pockets" of the planter. Taller selections, although less common, are superb cut flowers. They are better suited for informal cottage gardens or as filler in flower borders.

Ageratum is a good choice for containers. Here it is combined with shrimp plant, gerbera, and narrowleaf zinnia.

Photographers have noted a phenomenon that is specific to this plant and is often called the "ageratum effect." The blooms of ageratum do not appear blue in photographs. Even the bluest selections appear to be pinkish purple.

Planting and Care

Ageratum does not like hot, dry places. Make every effort to plant it in soil that is rich in organic matter and stays evenly moist, or consider planting something else. When planted in good soil and given fertilizer and regular watering, ageratum produces flowers nonstop from spring until the first fall frost. The blossoms are tiny, fluffy, and closely bunched and by the end of the season may completely blanket the foliage.

AT A GLANCE
❖

AGERATUM
Ageratum houstonianum

Features: blooms from spring until frost

Colors: blue, purple, pink, burgundy, white

Height: 6 to 24 inches

Light: full sun or light shade

Soil: well drained, fertile

Water: medium

Pests: whiteflies

Remarks: compact, very uniform, good for edging

While full sun yields the best show, afternoon shade will protect the thin-petaled blooms from scorching in the summer. The hairy, heart-shaped leaves are sensitive to cold and will blacken with the first frost—your signal to replace them with pansies or other cool-weather annuals if you have not already done so.

Ageratum has a vigorous, fibrous root system, and plants will often be rootbound when you buy them. Turn to page 21 to read about dealing with root-bound transplants. Set out transplants about two weeks after the last frost.

Different Selections

Blue is by far the most popular color of ageratum, and it can be found in many shades—sky blue, lavender, and violet blue. Ageratum can also be found in white and shades of pink and burgundy. Dwarf types, such as Blue Danube, Fine Wine, and True Blue, generally grow from 6 to 10 inches tall and spread 12 inches or more. Tall selections, such as Blue Horizon, grow about 24 inches tall and nearly as wide with long, sturdy stems that are perfect for cutting. They are also popular for drying and will hold their color; hang the cut stems upside down to dry.

Fall leaves contrast with ageratum's green, heart-shaped foliage and clusters of flowers.

Troubleshooting

Whiteflies, which are a common greenhouse pest, love this plant, so be sure the plants you bring home from the garden center are not infested. Even if the plants are clean, watch for whiteflies to appear in the garden in late spring and summer. See page 124 to read more about whiteflies.

Black-eyed Susan

Black-eyed Susan provides a familiar and friendly splash of color from mid- to late summer.

Black-eyed Susan is a gardener's delight; it is easy to grow, mixes well with other plants, and is a colorful addition to any setting. The blooms are 2 to 3 inches across and appear atop 3-foot stems from July until mid-September. Each bright yellow flower has a black cone or "eye" in its center, which gives the plant its name.

You can plant black-eyed Susan just about anywhere—in flower beds, among shrubs or ground cover, or in a cutting garden. Plant a grouping at the edge of a wood for a natural look. Because of its penetrating color, black-eyed Susan usually looks best when planted in groups, rather than scattered here and there.

As half-hardy perennials, black-eyed Susans may come back year after year, but this is unlikely. Instead, they usually grow leaves the first year and flower the second, much like biennials. They drop seed at the end of the season. You can often see black-eyed Susans colonizing fields and roadsides as a result of their prolific seeding.

Planting and Care

Black-eyed Susan grows best in moist, fertile soil, but the plants will tolerate poor, dry conditions. However, the soil must be well drained; in soggy soil, the roots will rot. Full sun produces bushier plants and more blooms, but flowers will also appear in light shade.

Sow seed directly in the garden in early spring, or start transplants indoors about six weeks before the last frost. Pat the seed into the soil so that it is in firm contact but not buried. When the seedlings sprout, thin to about 2 feet apart.

Black-eyed Susan often reseeds itself, so watch for seedlings. Young plants appear as a crown of fuzzy leaves that are similar to those of the parent plant. Dig and transplant seedlings in the spring.

This black-eyed Susan has narrow petals and a small eye for a dainty look.

AT A GLANCE

❖

BLACK-EYED SUSAN
Rudbeckia hirta

Features: vivid yellow blooms from mid- to late summer

Colors: bright yellow

Height: 24 to 36 inches

Light: full sun or light shade

Soil: well drained, fertile to poor

Water: low, wilts but comes back from drought

Pests: none specific

Remarks: reseeds easily

Different Selections

The flowers of all black-eyed Susans last for a long time, which makes them excellent cut flowers. Seed catalogs often list a strain of black-eyed Susan called gloriosa daisy. This plant has huge, bicolored blooms that are up to 7 inches across, with mahogany tones streaking toward the center. One selection of gloriosa daisy is called Pinwheel because of this unusual marking. The gloriosa daisy is especially valued for the impact its markings add to an arrangement of cut flowers, as is Irish Eyes, a selection noted for its green center.

Gloriosa daisy, a selection of black-eyed Susan, is prized for arrangements because of its artful markings.

Troubleshooting

Although not bothered by insects or diseases, plants may be knocked down by heavy rains. Be prepared to stake them by simply tying their stems to a 3- or 4-foot tomato stake.

Irish Eyes is an unusual selection with a green center.

IS IT ANNUAL OR PERENNIAL?

Perhaps the trickiest thing about black-eyed Susan is matching the name to the correct plant. A related species, *Rudbeckia fulgida,* is often erroneously called black-eyed Susan, but the correct name is orange cone-flower. However, orange cone-flower is fully perennial and does not reseed; it spreads by stems that grow from the base of the plant, and creep along the ground to form large masses of plants. Goldsturm is one of orange coneflower's most long-lived and popular selections.

Cabbage and Kale

Kale has frilly leaves that provide texture and color from fall until spring in areas with mild winters.

AT A GLANCE
❖
CABBAGE AND KALE
Brassica oleracea
var. *acephala*

Features: leafy, bright rosettes, excellent for borders

Colors: green with white to red centers

Height: 6 to 10 inches

Light: full sun

Soil: well drained, fertile

Water: low to medium

Pests: cabbageworms

Remarks: good color and texture in fall and winter

Hardy, colorful versions of culinary cabbage and kale, these ornamentals look like giant winter flowers. Their red, lavender, or white centers get brighter after the first frost. These cool-weather annuals thrive when temperatures drop, though they do not tolerate extreme cold. Gardeners in areas with mild winters should plant them in fall and winter for best color.

Use ornamental cabbage and kale in flower beds, pots, or even arrangements. Because they are large plants, cabbage and kale can be appreciated from a distance. Planted close together, they are a solid mass of color; placed in a curve around a mix of flowers, they become a handsome border.

Plant them with other cool-weather annuals, such as pansies and sweet William. The darkest shades are a great foil for blue, white, or yellow blooms. For a bold accent, mix these ornamentals singly with plants that have finely textured foliage, such as parsley. Plant them in masses in an unused portion of the vegetable garden to be harvested for tabletop arrangements and garnishes. Although edible, their flavor is inferior to that of culinary cabbage and kale.

Planting and Care

Nurseries may carry ornamental cabbage and kale in various sizes—small transplants, young plants in 4-inch pots, or mature plants in gallon containers. Plants growing in 4-inch pots or smaller can be set about a foot apart, as they will spread outward as they grow. Large plants, which are instant accents when planted, are not likely to spread after being set in the garden. Place mature plants closer together, so that the rosettes almost touch each other.

Plant in full sun for the best color, and keep the plants watered during dry weather. Although fairly tolerant of dry soil, young plants will not grow to full size without plenty of water. When given adequate water, sun, and fertilizer, small transplants will grow quickly. If the weather turns warm after they are in the ground, cabbage and kale may grow upward from the base and their normally short, hidden stems may grow a bit too long, so that the rosette seems to be sitting atop a tiny "trunk." If this happens, dig them up and replant deeper, right up to the base of the rosettes, so that the stem is buried.

The bright rosettes of ornamental cabbage and kale should be attractive through the winter unless the temperature regularly dips into the teens. In the spring, you will know that they are ready to be removed when the heads begin to grow tall. If left alone, they will stretch to about two feet tall and will grow a branched stalk of small yellow flowers. Culinary cabbages, collards, and other members of the cabbage family do the same. Some gardeners like the effect, leaving the plant in the garden until the flowers fade.

Different Selections

The leaves of ornamental cabbage and kale may be curly, smooth, or cut around the edges like a fringe. You will find curly-leafed kale and smooth-leafed cabbage in white and purplish pink, all growing about a foot in diameter. Cut-leafed kale, such as Peacock, has a more feathery texture than whole-leafed selections and is easier to knit together in masses. If you live in an area subject to sudden dips into the low teens, choose red-leafed selections; white ones are more likely to turn brown when they freeze.

Cut-leafed selections of kale have a feathery texture.

A full head of cabbage will be almost magenta after a series of frosts.

Starting from Seed

If you wish to grow your own transplants, sow the seed in late summer, about eight weeks before the first frost. It is both essential and difficult to keep the seedlings cool because you will be starting them during hot weather. Sow them indoors or under lights in a basement. Move the young transplants outside when the nights begin to cool in early fall.

Troubleshooting

Cabbage and kale are often bothered by cabbageworms—green velvety caterpillars that eat holes in the leaves. Turn to page 122 for more about cabbageworms.

Caladium

The vivid foliage of caladiums is as attractive as the blossoms of other annuals.

Caladiums are among the few annuals grown for their foliage, not their flowers. The large leaves color the summer garden with patterns of white, red, and green, bringing to it a fresh, cool feel. Caladiums thrive in heat but wither quickly in cool weather. However, from midspring until early fall, you will find them exceptionally easy to grow in shade; some also do well in full sun.

Because of their unique foliage, caladiums are strong visual elements in a garden. Their colors and textures add vivid contrast to a shade garden, brightening those areas not quite sunny enough for most flowering plants. Because they often grow to 24 inches tall, they can be used to fill large areas. For the best effect, try masses of a single selection, or plant two complementary colors under a tree, in an open planting bed, or along a garden path.

Planting and Care

Unlike other annuals, which are generally grown from seed, caladiums sprout from a bulblike tuber. In spring, you will find both transplants in pots and loose tubers for sale. When purchasing tubers, be aware of differences in size. Diameters range from 1 to 3½ inches. The larger the tuber, the fuller the plant will be, so always buy the largest ones available. They cost more but you will need fewer of them to have a full stand.

Large caladiums punctuate a formal planting of pink and white impatiens.

You can plant caladiums in the spring garden when the soil temperature has reached 70 degrees, usually three to four weeks after the last frost. If planted too early in the season, the tubers may rot.

Plant caladiums in soil that is rich, moist, and well drained. Place tubers 2 to 3 inches deep and 8 to 18 inches apart (depending on the leaf size of the selection). Place smaller tubers at about half the spacing of large ones; because they produce smaller plants, they will not need as much room to grow.

Caladiums need a lot of water, especially those in full sun. They wilt quickly and will go dormant if left too long without water. Mulch the soil around them to help retain moisture. During the summer, a *spathe*, or pointed flowering stalk, will sprout beneath the leaves; pinch these off when they appear, as flowering discourages the plant from producing more leaves.

Different Selections

There are two basic types of caladiums: fancy leafed and lance leafed. The only real difference between the two is the shape—the fancy leafed is heart shaped, while the lance leafed is arrow shaped. The range of colors and patterns extends from almost pure white Candidum to the burgundies of Irene Dank and Postman Joyner and a host of variegated selections. One of the most popular variegated

An elegant pot with caladiums and asparagus fern is a welcoming accent on this shaded terrace.

This mass planting of white Candidum brings light to a shady bed.

caladiums is Little Miss Muffet, a compact selection (about 10 inches tall) that bears green-and-white leaves with pink specks.

Often caladiums are considered suitable only for areas that have at least partial shade. Candidum Jr., Pink Symphony, and Gypsy Rose have a low tolerance to full sun and do best when planted in a shady location. Yet some will do quite well in full sun, especially Aaron, Lance Whorton, Red Frill, and Pink Cloud. Generally, the selections with thick leaves are more tolerant of sun than those with thin leaves.

Save the Tubers

Caladiums are killed by frost. Some gardeners will dig up the tubers before the first frost and save them to plant the following spring. To save the tubers, stop watering in early fall and allow the leaves to wither. Once the leaves are yellow and droopy, but before the first frost, dig up the tubers, dust off the soil, snip off the dying leaves, and air-dry in a shaded, well-ventilated area for several days. Pack them in dry sphagnum peat moss and store indoors at a temperature of about 70 degrees until the next year. You may also store the dry, healthy tubers in a mesh bag hung in a well-ventilated area.

Caladiums easily blend into existing plantings of ferns and hostas for added summer color.

A mix of caladiums and impatiens creates a stunning yet easy-to-grow shady border framed by lush ferns.

Calliopsis

This rugged annual, native throughout most of the United States, is often called plains coreopsis or golden tickseed. It is a 3-foot-tall, upright plant with long, wiry stems and divided leaves. Its yellow pinwheel flowers have vivid maroon centers; the name calliopsis means "beautiful eye." While tough enough to grow on the roadside and in the cracks of sidewalks, it is also graceful, lending a rich golden glow to problem areas of flower beds.

Calliopsis is excellent for meadows, street-side plantings, and other hot, hard-to-water places, as well as the lush conditions of a well-prepared flower bed. It looks superb in large groupings, creating a flowery blanket of color to fill a large area. It mixes nicely with other wildflowers, such as Queen Anne's lace, or with other summer annuals, including cosmos and mealycup sage. The tall stems make ideal cut flowers, staying crisp and pretty in a vase for more than a week.

Planting and Care

Calliopsis thrives on neglect and is often seen growing in highway medians. It is tolerant of every soil type: clay or sandy, acid or alkaline. Drainage is not important to these adaptable plants, as they will grow in soggy or dry conditions.

The plant develops a long central root that resents transplanting, so it is best to sow the seed directly in the garden. Thin seedlings to about 8 inches apart. For best flowering, plant in full sun anywhere you would like to see a drift of green, yellow, and maroon. Sow seed in the fall in the South and in spring farther north. Seed sown in the fall will produce green rosettes that will last through winter. Plants then grow taller in the spring, blooming for four to six weeks in early summer in the South and throughout the summer in cooler regions.

Remove spent blooms to encourage a longer period of bloom. Or, try shearing plants back; this often inspires a second round of flowers in early fall. If you want plants to reseed, however, leave the flowers to produce seeds. Calliopsis reseeds prolifically, and it will usually reappear on its own year after year. You can also save your own seeds to replant the next year.

Different Selections

You will see many types of coreopsis listed in catalogs; most are perennial. However, calliopsis is an annual and still grows in the wild; only a few named selections are available. Dwarf red plains coreopsis is a red plant that grows 12 to 24 inches tall and has solid crimson flowers.

Golden blossoms with mahogany-red centers are the signature of calliopsis, a great flower for seeding a meadow.

AT A GLANCE

❖

CALLIOPSIS
Coreopsis tinctoria

Features: heat-tolerant native with bright summer flowers

Colors: golden yellow with maroon centers

Height: 12 to 36 inches

Light: full sun

Soil: average to poor, acid to alkaline

Water: low to medium

Pests: none specific

Remarks: excellent cut flower

Celosia

The vibrant plumes of this celosia combine with its lime green foliage to add an exotic, tropical look to a summer garden.

P rized for its flamboyance in Victorian gardens, celosia remains popular today among gardeners who recognize its usefulness. Celosia is a reliable source of long-lasting, heat-tolerant color in mid-summer and early fall. The colors of its blooms range from warm pinks and creams to the hot tones of red, purple, and gold, and their unique forms are a delightful novelty.

Celosia ranges from 6 to 36 inches in height, with plume selections serving as a vertical accent in a flower bed or pot. Dwarf selections can be grouped to form a wave of color and texture at the front of a bed or border. Taller celosia can add interest to the back of a border or a rock garden, or the center of an island bed. Plant a large grouping for a dramatic effect, or use small groups, five to seven plants, to draw the eye to a bird bath, a fountain, or a water garden.

Taller selections of plumed celosia are an excellent choice for the center of a flower bed.

Different Selections

One type of celosia, Plumosa, is topped with an exotic plume that looks like a cluster of feathers. The Castle series, which stands 12 to 14 inches tall, has clusters of scarlet, yellow, or pink plumes; Apricot Brandy, a soft orange All-America Selections winner, grows to 16 inches tall. Plumed celosia is ideal as a background flower for low-growing bedding plants, such as ageratum or marigolds. Use a dwarf selection, such as the 6-inch Kimono, along a border.

The blooms of another celosia, Cristata, form a velvety crest. This plant is often called cockscomb because the crest resembles the comb of a rooster. Crested celosia is also used in beds and borders as a curiosity. Red Velvet, which has huge crimson blooms, or Jewel Box, dwarf 4- to 5-inch plants in red or gold, work well as a novelty when paired with other annuals.

Mass celosia in front of evergreen shrubs to spotlight its unusual blooms. Pair celosia with other flowers in borders; a tall crimson cockscomb, such as Floradale, looks great behind a mix of pink, purple, and white dwarf globe amaranth. A medium-sized plumed selection, such as Red Glow, will marry well with tall cosmos and daisies.

Growers have introduced wheat celosia, a Spicata hybrid, that is covered in small silvery-pink and purple spikes. Because it looks like a wildflower, this is an ideal annual for a naturalistic landscape, such as a rock garden. This annual has all the beauty of a wild grass with the bonus of elegant flowers. Selections of wheat celosia include Pink Candle, which bears rose-pink spikes, Flamingo Feather, a soft pink that fades to white, and Flamingo Purple, with purple plumes and dark reddish-green leaves. With its 3½-foot-tall stems and tapered spikes, wheat celosia is an excellent addition to both the landscape and the cutting garden.

Planting and Care

Hybrids grow best when started from transplants. They are difficult to start from seed because they must be kept uniformly warm and moist. Old-fashioned selections are less finicky and easier to grow from seed in the garden or in flats to be transplanted outdoors. Make sure you do not sow seeds or set out transplants until the soil temperature is warm, about two to three weeks after the last frost.

It is crucial not to set celosia out too early, as cool temperatures can stunt its growth. Give transplants plenty of room to branch; pinching the center of plumed blooms will encourage the plant to form many smaller "feathers" from side branches. (Do not pinch if you want to grow large plumes for cutting or drying.) Be sure celosia gets plenty of water throughout its early growth. If young hybrids are not properly watered, they will not bloom well once they mature.

Troubleshooting

Plants are occasionally bothered by powdery mildew, which looks like a white powder on the leaves. See page 123 for more about powdery mildew.

This hybrid, wheat celosia, looks like a wildflower and works well in naturalistic plantings.

FLOWERS FOR DRYING

Tall selections of plumed, crested, or wheat celosia are popular when dried for use in arrangements and crafts. Simply cut the flowers and hang them upside down for a week. The blooms last a long time and keep their color; after a year or so, they will fade to a pale, antiqued shade.

Coleus

Coleus foliage is as bright as a flower.

Coleus has so many shades of foliage that it is hard to believe the leaves are real. The leaves are every bit as showy as a flower. Coleus is available in reds, greens, copper, or white and provides a variation of texture as well as color in the garden. Best of all, it grows in the shade, where vivid color is hard to come by. However, many selections will also thrive in direct sun.

Coleus will brighten a wooded area with foliage that lasts until the first frost. One or two plants set among ferns in the shade will bring a nice spot of color to the green. It is also great along the north side of a house, where there is little direct sunlight, or as a filler in perennial beds, where it grows large and bushy and the color of its leaves never fades.

Planted in a pot or a hanging basket, coleus fills out quickly, making a neat, full plant. If a bed needs a summertime pick-me-up, remove the potted plant from its container and plant it directly in the garden, being sure to water it daily if needed until the roots become established.

AT A GLANCE
❖
COLEUS
Coleus x *hybridus*

Features: multicolored foliage from spring until frost

Colors: white, yellow, red to pink, copper, dark green to chartreuse, variegated combinations

Height: 6 inches to 3 feet

Light: full sun to shade

Soil: moist, fertile to poor

Water: medium to high, wilts but comes back from drought

Pests: none specific

Remarks: color rarely fades

Coleus is excellent for mixing with ferns and other finely textured foliage in shade.

Planting and Care

Coleus will not grow unless the weather is warm. A late frost will kill them, so do not be tempted to set plants out early. If you start with transplants, plant at least two weeks after the last frost. Tall selections can be kept fuller by pinching the tips of the stems every month or so as the plants grow. In late summer, coleus will send up spikes of small blue flowers, but to keep the plants full, pinch the flowers as they appear.

This large-leafed pink-and-green coleus punctuates a summer flower bed, bringing a contrast of texture as well as lasting color until frost.

From top: *Sunset Wizard, Golden Dragon*

Coleus does not require extra fertilizer through the season, but it will need plenty of water. Large-leafed selections may droop in summer heat and dry weather but they will recover quickly if you do not let them get completely dry.

Different Selections

Perhaps the most perplexing aspect of growing coleus is choosing a selection, as they vary greatly in appearance. Coleus spans from 6 inches to nearly 3 feet in height, and its leaves may be small and lobed or large and full. Color is also an issue, as coleus comes in a rainbow of shades. The Carefree series are dwarf, bushy plants that may be easily recognized by their small, lobed leaves. These plants are excellent for small pots, as they grow only 8 to 12 inches tall. Wizard is another popular series; these plants grow 1 to 2 feet tall and have heart-shaped leaves.

The leaves of some selections will lose their color in full sun, especially in dry climates. If you know your coleus will be in sun all day, look for selections which have been especially bred to tolerate the sun, such as Alabama Sunset. The Sunlovers series includes selections that will grow in full sun; these do not flower in summer, so there is no need to pinch the leaves. Plum Parfait and Burgundy Sun are dark reds that will tolerate full sun. Red Ruffles, Cranberry Salad, Freckles, and Rustic Orange will grow in either full sun or shade.

Starting from Seed

Gardeners sometimes choose to grow coleus from seed if a particular color is not available at local garden centers. You can grow transplants by starting seeds indoors six to eight weeks before the last frost date. Gently pat them into the seed-starting mix with your fingertips to be sure that they are not buried, as the seeds need light to germinate. For best germination, keep the soil at 70 degrees or slightly warmer. (Turn to page 22 to read more about starting from seed.)

Red Wizard

Cosmos

This annual's name was derived from the Greek word kosmos, *which means "beautiful thing."*

Cosmos can be a gardener's best friend in late summer, when other plants are fading. This carefree annual boasts charming blooms in two dazzling color ranges: lustrous pink, rose, and white; and radiant yellow, orange, and tomato red. It is so easy to grow that you need only sow the seed in a sunny place and watch this fast-growing, sun-loving plant thrive.

Common cosmos, *Cosmos bipinnatus,* offers billowy, fernlike foliage and 4-inch-wide, daisylike flowers. It does well in mass plantings or near the back of a border, where it can grow to 4 to 5 feet in height. Pair it with hollyhocks, fall veronicas, or purple coneflower for comely combinations. Klondyke cosmos, *Cosmos sulphureus,* is sometimes called yellow cosmos or orange cosmos and bears a smaller bloom than *Cosmos bipinnatus.* Dwarf selections of Klondyke cosmos are ideal for the front of a border or bed, or as a container plant, especially when mixed with plants that have more dense foliage, such as English ivy or creeping lantana.

Cosmos is often grown for its dependability as a cut flower. Once you get accustomed to having these informal bouquets in your home, they will become a summer tradition. Another plus for cosmos is that it blooms until the first frost, extending its colorful presence well into the fall garden. Klondyke cosmos attracts bees and butterflies, and, when it sets seed, goldfinches. Klondyke cosmos has sparse foliage, so plant it behind short, dense plants to conceal its leggy stems.

The soft color of cosmos makes it a delightful transitional annual.

Planting and Care

Both types of cosmos are easy to sow directly in the garden. When sown in spring, cosmos grows in poor to average soil, tolerating heat and humidity, and blooms in just 10 to 12 weeks. Scatter seeds on the ground without burying them. Sow in well-drained soil in full sun after all danger of frost is past. Once plants are established, they will tolerate high temperatures and dry spells. Do not overfertilize or plant in rich soil, or you will get a lot of foliage but few flowers.

AT A GLANCE

❖

COMMON COSMOS
Cosmos bipinnatus

Features: heat-tolerant annual with daisylike flowers

Colors: white, pink, lavender, rose

Height: 2 to 5 feet

Light: full sun

Soil: well drained, poor to fertile

Water: low

Pests: none specific

Remarks: dependable color, grown as a cut flower

Cosmos has thin stems that often require staking. You should pinch plants early in the season to encourage growth. To keep both types of cosmos blooming, cut flowers back as they fade, if you are not cutting them to bring indoors. Klondyke cosmos blooms on long, wiry stems; you can cut the plants back to a foot high in midsummer to encourage a fresh flush of flowers.

Different Selections

Common cosmos features the award-winning Sonata series, which are compact, grow to 20 to 24 inches tall, and bloom in white or a mix of white, pink, and rose with charming yellow eyes. Sensation Mixed is another favorite, with crimson, pink, and white blooms on wispy 4-foot-tall stems.

Klondyke selections include the Lady Bird series, compact, early-blooming plants that grow to a foot tall and bear semidouble flowers in orange and yellow. Sunny Red is a 2-foot-tall All-America Selections winner with bright scarlet, single flowers that soften to orange as they mature. Bright Lights Mixed bears early, semidouble flowers in a mix of yellow, gold, orange, and scarlet on 3-foot-tall stems. Diablo, another All-America Selections winner, has orange-red flowers on an 18- to 24-inch plant.

Starting from Seed

You may also grow your own transplants about five to seven weeks before the last frost. Because the plants reseed so easily, you can encourage a second crop in the same year by letting some of the first flowers that appear produce seed. Seeds that drop to the ground will germinate and grow quickly in warm summer weather.

On a sunny day, the blossoms of Klondyke cosmos have a near-fluorescent glow.

AT A GLANCE
❖
KLONDYKE COSMOS
Cosmos sulphureus

Features: upright annual covered with daisylike flowers

Colors: yellow, gold, orange, crimson

Height: 1 to 3 feet

Light: full sun

Soil: well drained, poor to average

Water: low

Pests: none specific

Remarks: great cut flower, attracts butterflies and goldfinches

Pinwheels of color brighten a midsummer garden as the wiry stems of Klondyke cosmos billow out from a wooden fence.

Dusty Miller

Dusty miller's silvery hue glows in moonlight.

The frosty foliage of dusty miller seems to have been created simply to make other plants look good. The silvery hue of this modest plant enhances the plants around it, intensifying the colors of adjacent blossoms and the green of nearby leaves. It brings soft, cool color and fine, feathery texture to beds, borders, and containers.

For a pleasing contrast, plant dusty miller against a backdrop of brightly colored annuals, such as yellow marigolds. For a softer effect, pair it with pink, purple, or blue blooms, such as sweet William, petunia, or globe amaranth. Or plant it at the front of a perennial bed at the base of an evergreen border. To separate brightly colored flowers in a bed, plant dusty miller as a transition between different hues, neutralizing the contrast. Compact selections are great for edging an herb garden or brightening rock gardens and containers, where they mix well with just about any flower.

Dusty miller foliage shows up well under moonlight and other night lighting, which makes it a good companion for plantings near decks, patios, or walkways. Its woolly texture also adds to its appeal, as children like to touch the fuzzy leaves.

Dusty miller makes an excellent edging for an evergreen border, with its gray-green foliage bringing out the richness of surrounding colors.

AT A GLANCE
❖
DUSTY MILLER
Senecio cineraria

Features: woolly, old-fashioned plant prized for its foliage

Colors: silver, gray green

Height: 6 to 12 inches

Light: full sun to very light shade

Soil: well drained

Water: low

Pests: none specific

Remarks: very drought tolerant

Planting and Care

Dusty miller is a perennial in the Lower South but may be treated as an annual farther north. Plants may be started from seeds or transplants and may be planted up to two months before the first fall frost, as it will tolerate freezing weather. Choose a sunny area of well-drained, slightly sandy soil. If you sow seed directly in the garden, do not cover; they need light to germinate.

Dusty miller is drought tolerant, but you need to keep new plants watered until they are well established. Remove the yellow flowers that appear in May and June to keep foliage looking its best until fall. Midway through the season, dusty miller may get leggy; if so, cut the plants back to about half their height to encourage branching and more compact growth. In areas where it is perennial, cut it back to the ground in late winter before new growth begins.

Different Selections

Silver Queen makes a nice choice for garden borders, growing only 8 inches tall. Another option is Silver Dust, which reaches 9 to 12 inches in height and bears fine, lacy foliage. Cirrus is a compact plant with lobed leaves that grows from 6 to 8 inches tall. Silver Lace is really a different species, *Chrysanthemum ptarmiciflorum,* that you will also see labeled as dusty miller. It has very fine, lacy foliage and grows 24 inches tall, making a nice addition to a large container.

Both drought and sun tolerant, dusty miller finds a perfect summer home in containers, where it is forgiving lest you forget to water.

55

Four O'Clock

The trumpetlike four o'clock is easy to grow.

This annual is covered with trumpet-shaped blooms that open in late afternoon—around four o'clock—from midsummer until the first frost. The plants are a fragrant addition to the summer garden and are especially nice for gardeners who are away from home until late afternoon each day. Colorful and easy to grow, this fast-growing annual will develop into a small shrub by midsummer. Known for centuries as the Marvel of Peru, old-fashioned four o'clock continues to amaze gardeners with its reliable ability to "tell time" and perfume the air as the sun wanes.

Four o'clocks have heavy, multibranched stems and medium-sized leaves; they look a bit like small shrubs by midsummer. Use four o'clocks anywhere you need to fill a gap with a 2- to 3-foot-tall flowering shrub, such as near a new foundation, in a sunny, mixed border, at steps leading to a deck or porch, or along a fence or other structure. It also makes an excellent low hedge or screen for an informal cottage garden. Use it to fill any bare space where you can enjoy its nighttime bouquet. Children will enjoy watching four o'clocks open and release their lemony, sweet scent, a dependable part of every afternoon.

Planting and Care

A tender perennial in the Lower and Coastal South and warmer portions of the Middle South, four o'clock is more frequently grown as a hardy annual. It returns each summer from seed without any encouragement on your part.

New plants are easy to start from seed, but the seeds are tough, so soak them for a few hours before planting to allow seedlings to break through more easily. After all threat of frost is past, sow seeds about ¼ inch deep in full sun or light shade in well-drained soil. Or, start seeds indoors four to six weeks before the last frost.

If you have a friend or neighbor with four o'clocks, you can dig up and divide the tubers in the fall, store them in a cool dry place during the winter, and plant them in the spring. Set out tubers or transplants 24 inches apart. In warmer regions of the South, the tubers are winter-hardy and plants will be perennial. After the second year, the plant will spread by tubers, popping up several inches away

---

AT A GLANCE

❖

FOUR O'CLOCK
Mirabilis jalapa

Features: old-fashioned annual covered with fragrant, tubular blooms

Colors: red, pink, yellow, violet, multicolored

Height: 2 to 3 feet

Light: full sun to light shade

Soil: well drained

Water: medium

Pests: Japanese beetles

Remarks: self-sows, perfumes the night air

from the original. Seedlings may also sprout nearby. Farther north, the only way to have four o'clocks year after year is to save the tubers or let the flowers reseed.

Different Selections

Many gardeners do not know what selection they have in their gardens because they got their seed from a friend or it appeared naturally. Jingles is a named selection with bicolored flowers. Often seeds are just sold as Mixed, meaning a variety of colors—usually pink, yellow, orange, white, and red— are contained in the packet.

Troubleshooting

Four o'clocks may be bothered by Japanese beetles. Turn to page 123 for more about this pest.

A floral timepiece, four o'clock opens every afternoon just before suppertime with a colorful mix of blooms.

Foxglove

For an elegant touch, plant shorter selections in an urn or other large container placed beside your home's entry or on a terrace.

Few plants rival the spires of foxglove for adding stately drama to a bed or border. Easy to grow from transplants, foxgloves are a pleasure not to be missed, whether you enjoy their colorful embroidery from a distance or the charm of their freckled blossoms up close.

Foxgloves boast large, bell-shaped blooms in colors ranging from white, yellow, and shell pink to lavender, magenta and deep rose. Plant them wherever you need a tall bloom and want to draw attention. They can be spectacular in a border, in a showy corner, around the mailbox, even in a container.

Planting and Care

Foxgloves enjoy partial shade and moist, well-drained soil. If you have sand or hard clay, add plenty of organic matter before you plant. Space plants 12 to 18 inches apart to allow room for the foliage to expand.

Foxgloves are biennial, growing leaves one year and blooming the next. Look for plants in quart containers (or larger) with six or more large leaves to set out in fall for blooms the following spring. In most of the South, transplants set out in the fall will remain a handsome rosette of foliage through winter. Farther north or during hard winters, freezes may knock back the foliage but will not hurt the roots.

In the spring, the flower stalk rockets skyward until it stands 2 to 7 feet tall, depending upon the selection. It is best to enjoy foxgloves from late April through June; then replace the plants after they flower with summer annuals.

AT A GLANCE
❖
FOXGLOVE
Digitalis purpurea

Features: tall spires of pastel spring blooms

Colors: white, yellow, pink, purple

Height: 2 to 7 feet

Light: morning sun or partial shade

Soil: fertile, well drained

Water: medium

Pests: spider mites

Remarks: top choice for drama in spring

You may find mature plants for sale at garden centers in late winter or early spring; these may bloom the first year, depending on their size and how early you set them out. If not, they will certainly bloom the next spring.

Different Selections

Whether you buy plants locally or order seed through the mail, you will find several selections. Excelsior Hybrids are probably the most popular, growing in a mixture of white, pink, and purple. Although the stalks are quite strong, the plants will grow 5 to 7 feet tall and can get heavy when the flowers are fully open. Be prepared to stake these taller selections, as spring storms may otherwise destroy a beautiful display.

Foxy Mixed is an All-America Selections winner that blooms quickly, often in the first season if planted in fall in the South or in spring in the North. It is smaller than the more popular foxgloves, with a single majestic spike that is supposed to grow only 3 feet high but generally exceeds that height in the South. Tall foxgloves will produce many smaller spikes if you snip them back in the spring as the rosette begins to sprout a stalk.

Cutting

Foxgloves make fine additions to a spring bouquet of cut flowers. Cutting is also a good way to control exceptionally tall plants. By the time the tip of the stalk begins to bloom, the lower portions are producing ripening seeds. If you cut off the stalk at this point, the plant will usually sprout more spikes, although they are never as big or as showy as the first ones. If you leave the seeds, the plants may self-sow, reseeding themselves so that they produce new seedlings each year.

Troubleshooting

In the summer, foxgloves may become weak and bedraggled when spider mites attack the foliage. Rather than spraying, it is easier to pull up the plants each spring, replace them with summer annuals, and then plant strong, new foxgloves in fall. Turn to page 124 to read more about spider mites.

A foreground of pansies is perfect for shorter selections of foxglove.

In spring, foxgloves stand tall with exquisite bold spires, drawing attention to themselves and giving a strong vertical accent to a flower garden.

Geranium

No matter where they grow, geraniums are easily recognized from a distance. Their brightly colored blooms grow in clusters on long stems that stand above abundant foliage. Though they will grow when planted in the garden, geraniums are especially suited to containers. Almost like a pedestal, a pot elevates the blooms, increasing the impact of their showy clusters. Make the most of these vivid blooms by using geraniums to accent an entry, pinpoint a fountain or other garden feature, grace a table, or fill a window box.

Planting and Care

Most geraniums can only be started from cuttings and transplants. Those grown from seed (often called seed geraniums) are very difficult to start at home. Unless you have a greenhouse, begin with purchased transplants. Geraniums need full sun and well-drained, fertile soil that stays moist. Never let the soil in the bed or the container dry, or the leaves will begin to turn yellow; on the other hand, do not let the soil stay soggy or the roots will rot. When potting geraniums (or any annual) in a container, buy a soil mix that is pH balanced. In a pot or in a flower bed, you should raise the pH to about 6.5 by adding lime, as most geraniums do not like strongly acid soil.

In the South, geraniums appreciate some shade in the afternoon. However, whether they receive afternoon shade or not, many selections will slow down or stop producing blooms until the nights cool down in late August or September. Just keep them watered and fertilized, and you will be pleased by their revival in the fall. To encourage the production of new blooms, remove old flowers as they fade and use a bloom-boosting fertilizer, such as 15-30-15, which contains the proper ratio of nitrogen to phosphorus and potassium.

AT A GLANCE

❖

GERANIUM
Pelargonium x *hortorum*

Features: bright spots of color from early summer to frost

Colors: white, pink, scarlet, salmon, orange, lavender

Height: 12 to 25 inches

Light: full sun, afternoon shade

Soil: well drained, fertile

Water: medium to high

Pests: whiteflies

Remarks: great for mass plantings, pots, window boxes

Different Selections

The most popular geraniums grow from 18 to 25 inches tall and bear attractive, lily-pad-shaped foliage. The leaves often vary in hue and may have a dark ring. To avoid a summer pause of blooms in the South, try selections known to be less susceptible to heat. These include the Orbit series, the Pinto series, the Americana series, and Freckles, an All-America Selections winner. These selections are vigorous and have a fuller habit, which allows them to tolerate tough Southern summers.

Dynamo and Elite are compact plants with plentiful blooms. A few geraniums, such as Marilyn, Grace, and Judy, have a habit that is low and spreading and may be used as a seasonal ground cover. They are also good for hanging baskets, window boxes, or hayracks hung on the rails of a deck.

Occasionally you will see geraniums called Floribunda, which refers to the free flowering of many of the types started from seed. Generally they have small, simple blooms rather than giant lollipop-like double blooms. Those with giant double flowers are spectacular, but their petals tend to hang on as the flowers fade and turn an unsightly brown.

Ivy-leafed geraniums *(Pelargonium peltatum)*, which have trailing stems and ivylike leaves, are the least heat tolerant of geraniums. Although they do well through summer in cooler climates, they struggle in the South. If you buy these in spring for a basket or window box, be prepared to nurse them through a hot summer with plenty of water; they will be dormant through summer but should enjoy a revival in the fall. In Florida and South Texas, they are grown as winter annuals.

Troubleshooting

Whiteflies are a major pest of geraniums. To avoid introducing whiteflies to your garden, be sure to buy plants that are not infested. See page 124 for more about whiteflies.

Some geraniums produce smaller blooms, but they bear more of them than the large-flowered types.

Globe Amaranth

Globe amaranth is valued for its intense color. The papery blossoms are also attractive to skipper butterflies.

Globe amaranth is prized for its ability to produce hundreds of colorful, cloverlike blooms that hardly ever fade, even in mid-summer. Undaunted by heat, each flower glows like a candle lit in purple, pink, white, orange, or red. Globe amaranth is also valued for its use as a dried flower; upon close inspection, the flowers appear to be made of rice paper. When cut at the peak of their color, the papery blooms retain their pigment for up to a year, making globe amaranth a popular choice for dried arrangements, wreaths, and other crafts.

Use globe amaranth in flower beds, for edgings, or in containers. Dwarf types make excellent choices for pots and window boxes because they are compact and drought tolerant. Any selection will work nicely in front of taller annuals, such as Queen Anne's lace. For brilliant contrast, combine purple globe amaranth with the yellow of black-eyed Susan or the orange of narrowleaf zinnia. For a softer look, try lavender selections with blue ageratum or silver dusty miller. In addition to being visually attractive, the blooms of globe amaranth also attract butterflies.

Planting and Care

You can plant globe amaranth in the spring from transplants or from seed sown directly in the garden. Sow seeds in full sun in well-drained soil. Globe amaranth does not grow well in soggy soil but is tolerant of poor, sandy soil or heavy clay as long as it has adequate drainage.

If you set out transplants, do so in spring after all danger of frost has passed. Water the young plants regularly for the first few weeks; after that, the plants need no attention other than occasional watering during periods of extended drought. Globe amaranth will reseed; look for seedlings to reappear in the garden next spring.

If you want to dry globe amaranth blossoms, cut the stems before the flowers have fully opened and hang them upside down in a well-ventilated room.

Different Selections

There are many different selections of globe amaranth. Buddy is a short, compact plant (10 to 12 inches tall) with white or purple blooms and is suited for flower beds and containers. Dwarf White and Gnome produce neat, petite plants that grow only 8 to 10 inches tall. Taller selections are better for cutting, growing about 2½ feet tall, and include Lavender Lady, Pomponette Pink, and Pomponette

White. Strawberry Fields is a tall, bright red globe amaranth. Tall selections tend to flop over after a hard rain but do not need to be staked—they will stand up on their own.

Starting from Seed

You may need to start your own transplants to assure that you grow the color of blooms you want. Soak the seeds overnight and sow indoors 8 to 10 weeks before the last frost. Be patient; seeds of globe amaranth are slow to germinate but will sprout in two to three weeks in soil that is warm (70 to 75 degrees).

There are many selections of globe amaranth, including this red one, Strawberry Fields.

Purple and pink globe amaranth last from summer through fall. Here they are combined with perennial Autumn Joy sedum.

Hollyhock

Double-flowered hollyhocks add dramatic color to a midsummer garden.

AT A GLANCE
❖
HOLLYHOCK
Alcea rosea

Features: tall, dramatic, old-fashioned accents in midsummer

Colors: yellow, white, pink, red, maroon, copper, purple

Height: 2 to 8 feet

Light: full sun

Soil: fertile to poor, well drained

Water: medium to high

Pests: rust, caterpillars, spider mites, Japanese beetles

Remarks: needs to be staked

The quintessential English garden flowers, hollyhocks are popular for their romance and nostalgia, as well as their strong vertical presentation. Beginning in early summer, they rise to 8 feet tall, with the upper portions of their stalks cheerfully loaded with colorful, paperlike blooms measuring 3 to 6 inches across.

Dramatic in both size and shape, hollyhocks will draw attention wherever they are planted. They are stately when added to the back of a border or charming as foundation plantings for a country home. Hollyhocks also work well as colorful screens and are terrific accents for beds or wildflower gardens.

Plant hollyhocks in groups in front of a wall or a weathered fence, against the sunny side of a deck, or around the mailbox. Hollyhocks are easy to grow and and fun for children, as taller selections will surpass them in height. As an added bonus, your plants may also be visited by hummingbirds.

Planting and Care

Hollyhocks are often labeled perennial but are grown as annuals or biennials in most areas. They are very susceptible to diseases and pests and usually need to be pulled up by the end of the season.

You may start plants from seed or from transplants. Choose a sunny spot with well-drained soil. Sow seeds or set out transplants in the fall in the Coastal, Lower, and Middle South. Farther north, plant in spring when the soil can be easily worked. Hollyhocks thrive in sun and do not mind heat, but the huge blooms and thick leaves need regular watering.

Different Selections

There are many different selections of hollyhock, ranging from 2 to 8 feet tall. Traditional hollyhocks bear single blooms, while newer selections have frilled, double blooms. Powderpuff Mixed features 4-inch-wide red, white, yellow, or pink double blooms on 5-foot-tall shrubby plants. Fordhook Giants Mixed offers masses of colorful double flowers on 6-foot stalks. Character's Double Mixed produces 6- to 8-foot plants that also bear double blooms in an array of colors from white, yellow, and pink to red, maroon, and copper. Alcea Country Garden Mixed brings back old-fashioned single blooms that add charm to informal gardens in a wide range of colors.

Show off the architectural qualities of hollyhocks by placing them in front of a wall or other structure. Here they are accompanied by another old-fashioned favorite, larkspur.

Troubleshooting

Hollyhocks are susceptible to hollyhock rust, a fungal disease that develops on the underside of the leaves and weakens the plant. Allow plenty of spacing between plants for good air circulation as a preventive measure. Hollyhocks can also fall victim to caterpillars, Japanese beetles, and spider mites, especially in hot climates. Be prepared to spray them several times. See pages 122–124 for more about these pests.

Impatiens

Healthy impatiens are covered with blooms from spring until fall.

Blooming nonstop from spring until the first frost, impatiens find their way into more gardens than any other summer annual. Low-maintenance, tropical hybrids, they needs only a few hours of sun to produce dazzling mounds of flowers for five to seven months. Impatiens come in more than 15 different colors—from shimmering whites and pale pinks to vivid purples and bright oranges. Faithful bloomers in the shade, impatiens are by far America's best-selling bedding plants.

You can use this versatile annual to enliven evergreen shrub borders or mass it for waves of color. You can also set out a few plants to strategically fill holes in shade gardens, or let impatiens colorfully cascade from hanging baskets and containers near an entry, a terrace, or a deck. Impatiens work well as a ground cover in woodland settings, mixed with ferns, caladiums, and other shade lovers for a cool effect.

AT A GLANCE

❖

IMPATIENS
Impatiens wallerana and
New Guinea hybrids

Features: nonstop blooms from spring until frost

Colors: white, pink, lavender, orange, red, purple

Height: 6 to 24 inches

Light: shade to partial shade, morning sun

Soil: moist but well drained

Water: high, wilts in afternoon, keep soil evenly moist

Pests: slugs

Remarks: New Guinea impatiens tolerate full sun, all impatiens grow well in partial shade

Planting and Care

The easiest way to start impatiens is to purchase transplants after the last frost. However, in wooded areas, you may choose to scatter the fine seed directly in the garden. Often impatiens reseed themselves, although the offspring will not always look like the originals.

Plant impatiens in the shade or in areas that are shaded in the afternoon. Although many selections can tolerate sun, they will need an excessive amount of water during the summer. No matter where they grow, impatiens will need a lot of water during dry spells. Be sure to provide adequate moisture and they will bloom profusely until the fall.

You do not need to pinch blooms to keep impatiens continuously blooming. However, you may need to fertilize them a second time during the season if the leaves turn light green.

When impatiens seedpods are ripe and full, the slightest touch will cause them to burst, scattering seeds to the wind. You can save seeds for the next year by storing them in a dry glass jar. To save a particular plant over winter, you may take cuttings or move the plants indoors before the first frost. Once they are rooted, plant them in pots on a sunny windowsill. Remember that the offspring will bear blooms of different colors than those of the original plants.

A multicolored mix is one of the most popular ways to plant impatiens.

Starting from Seed

It is easier to start impatiens from transplants, but if you want to grow them from seed, remember that the seed is very fine, so sow carefully. Use a salt shaker to make the tiny seeds easier to spread over the bed, and be sure to keep the area watered.

Though considered difficult to germinate, the seed of impatiens sprout quickly if properly cared for. Sow seed six to eight weeks before the last spring frost. The seeds need light to germinate, so never cover. Instead, pat them gently into contact with the soil. Keep the seeds moist so that they do not dry out; at a temperature between 70 and 75 degrees, seedlings will sprout in about 10 days. Transfer the seedlings to small pots. When they are about 3 inches tall, you can set them in the garden, about 18 inches apart. (Turn to page 22 for more about seed starting.)

Most New Guinea impatiens do not grow well from seed. Selections that can be grown from seed include Tango and Spectra.

In shady spots, impatiens bloom profusely, complementing neighboring ferns and softening the hard edges of pavement.

New Guinea Impatiens

The introduction of new hybrid impatiens, derived from plants found in New Guinea in 1970, brought a new look to American gardens. With dark, variegated foliage, bigger flowers, and the ability to tolerate full sun, New Guinea impatiens have found their way into flower beds, borders, and hanging baskets across the country.

New Guinea impatiens range from 18 to 26 inches tall and sport lush leaves that may be green, red, or variegated. They have more upright stems than other impatiens and their blooms are twice the size. In addition to their large, cheerful blooms, these hybrids are outstanding for their lush, colorful foliage, and this color must be considered when using New Guinea impatiens in mixed plantings. For example, Constellation has green-and-yellow leaves, while Star War features dark red foliage.

New Guinea impatiens are patented and are propagated from cuttings rather than seeds, so the plants are generally more expensive than other impatiens. However, New Guinea impatiens grow larger than common impatiens, so you should space them 2 feet apart. Thus you will need fewer transplants to fill a bed.

The variegated leaves and lavender flowers of this New Guinea impatiens are a bright foil to dark evergreens.

Different Selections

New selections of impatiens are being continuously developed, so there are many different forms, sizes, and colors available to gardeners. Dwarf types are great for hanging baskets and groundcovers in shady and wooded settings. The Twinkle series produces bicolored flowers with a white central star, and the Super Elfin series comes in many solid colors.

There are dwarf versions of the ever-popular Elfins. Growing about a foot tall in the South, they are very full and spill nicely over the edge of a container. Medium-height impatiens, which are 3 to 4 inches taller than the dwarfs, include the bicolored Ripples series, Tangeglow with bright orange flowers, and Blitz, which has red blooms with bronze foliage and was the first impatiens to win an All-America Selections award.

Among taller impatiens (18 inches and up), look for the Grand series and the Imp series, both with many solid colors. For double-flowered impatiens, which look like tiny roses, consider Fancifrills.

Troubleshooting

Impatiens branch from the base so they seldom grow leggy. However, in the South, plants may grow a third taller than the height stated on the label because they continue to grow during warm nights. To trim them back, snip the tips by no more than one-third. Also, remember that impatiens growing in full morning sun with plenty of water may grow twice as tall as the same selection that gets only an hour of sun per day and less water. Keep this in mind when you choose your selections and planting locations.

Impatiens are often bothered by slugs. Turn to page 124 to read about control of these pests.

Impatiens branch at the base to form dense, compact plants.

Lantana

Lantana softens the landscape with exuberant foliage and masses of bright flowers that attract butterflies.

From spring until the first freeze, lantana colors the garden with clusters of small flowers that range from bright yellow and orange to pastel rose, lavender, and white. Certain selections behave like chameleons, with their tiny flowers fading and changing color from day to day. Its dependable flowering, teamed with its lovely form and tough, woody nature, make lantana hard to beat as a summer accent plant.

Lantana is actually a tropical shrub and will produce long branches. Some selections creep while others arch upward. Creeping types grow about 1 foot tall and 3 feet wide. The larger arching types may grow to 4 feet tall and equally wide. Both may be planted to soften the hard edges of the landscape, such as marking a patio corner or spilling over a rock wall. This annual is great for the front of the border or as a summer ground cover. You will also appreciate lantana for its ability to attract butterflies.

AT A GLANCE
❖

LANTANA
Lantana species

Features: bouquet-like clusters of small flowers from summer to fall

Colors: yellow, rose, lavender, orange

Height: 1 to 4 feet tall

Light: full sun

Soil: well drained, average

Water: low to medium

Pests: spider mites, whiteflies

Remarks: forgiving of heat, excellent for containers

Lantana's creeping or trailing nature makes it perfect for retaining walls and raised beds.

Planting and Care

Set out plants in full sun about two weeks after the last frost. Lantana tolerates poor, sandy soil or clay when provided good drainage. It blooms profusely, even in the hottest weather, and is often perennial in the Lower and Coastal South. Water well during extended dry spells to keep the dark green foliage from wilting.

You may overwinter potted lantana indoors in a sunroom or cool garage, but be prepared to control spider mites and whiteflies. Trim the plant back a few weeks before spring planting to encourage branching and fullness.

Different Selections

Lantana *(Lantana camara)* is sold for containers and shrub beds. Most selections grow 3 to 4 feet tall. Radiation, whose flower clusters are yellow, then orange and red, often sports all three colors at the same time. Pink Caprice produces a combination of pink and yellow flower clusters. Dazzler is a tricolor of delicate pink, yellow, and white with an abundance of large flowers. Miss Huff is a more cold-hardy selection that is perennial through the warmer parts of the Middle South. Lemon Swirl is a smaller, 12- to 18-inch plant with variegated leaves, pale yellow flowers, and a strong scent.

Trailing lantana *(Lantana montevidensis)* is a cascading plant that grows from 12 to 30 inches (depending on the selection). It is popular for containers and hanging baskets where its lilac flowers bloom in profusion. Its stems are thin and lie flat, creeping along the ground or dangling from a basket or over a wall. Try White Lightnin' or Lavender Swirl, or use both together in a basket.

Troubleshooting

Lantana is bothered by spider mites and whiteflies. Spider mites are at their worst during dry weather in spring and fall. Whiteflies usually appear from mid- to late summer. Both pests will cause the leaves to turn a sickly yellow. Turn to page 124 for more information about spider mites and whiteflies.

This lantana's radiant tricolored blossoms are cheerful and attractive to the eye.

Larkspur

Admired for its cool colors and graceful spires, larkspur makes an excellent cut flower.

AT A GLANCE

❖

LARKSPUR
Consolida species

Features: mid- to late spring annual with tall, handsome spires of color

Colors: white, pink, rose, red, blue, lavender, salmon

Height: 1 to 5 feet

Light: full sun to partial shade

Soil: loose, well drained

Water: medium

Pests: slugs

Remarks: excellent cut or dried flower

Sprouting from seed while the weather is cool, larkspur is a charming addition to the spring garden with its old-fashioned colors, airy foliage, and graceful flowering spikes. Amid clouds of light green stems and leaves, 2- to 4-foot-tall spikes shoot up with pink, deep blue, white, and lavender blooms. Though similar in appearance to delphinium, larkspur is easier to grow, especially in the South, where it reseeds and returns annually in a reliable burst of color.

Use larkspur in the middle or back of a border, against a fence, or in a meadow or cutting garden. Its traditional color scheme—pink, white, and blue—mixes beautifully with roses. Blue larkspur brings out the sunny side of golden marigolds, poppies, and calliopsis. Newer salmon colors are lovely with white daisies. When planted with spring-blooming bulbs, larkspur will emerge to conceal the leaves and stems of the other plants with its own fernlike foliage. Larkspur also fills in gaps between spring and summer perennials in a bed. If interplanted with summer-blooming cosmos, the cosmos will bloom furiously as the larkspur finally fades in summer heat.

For centuries, gardeners have enjoyed larkspur for its elegance as a cut flower. Because it retains its rich colors after drying, it is also used in arrangements of dried flowers.

Planting and Care

Larkspur grows best when started from seed directly sown in loose, well-drained soil in full sun or partial shade. In the South, sow larkspur seeds in the fall after the soil has cooled, as seeds will not germinate at temperatures above 70 degrees; plants will sprout in fall and wait through winter, resuming growth with each warm spell as spring approaches. Even if the seeds do not sprout, sowing seed in fall gives plants a chance to sprout early in the spring, which promotes longer flowering. Farther north, you should sow seeds in early spring as soon as the soil is workable. This annual enjoys cool weather when given ample water.

Larkspur is difficult, but not impossible, to transplant. If you want to grow your own transplants, sow seeds in 4-inch pots (one seed per pot) so that the roots will not be disturbed when you transplant them. Place the pots in a cool area. Seeds are slow to germinate, taking about four weeks, so start them six to eight weeks prior to setting out seedlings. Do not start seeds too early; seedlings should be young (1 to 2 inches tall) when transplanted.

Provided the right conditions, larkspur will thrive and reseed from year to year. In times of drought, water once a week. Do not let the plants dry out. In the South, larkspur will begin to fade as the weather warms in June, but if you keep it well watered, it will persist a few more weeks.

Different Selections

Larkspur is accurately known by the name *Consolida*, with different species, such as *Consolida ambigua*, branching larkspur, and *Consolida orientalis*, rocket larkspur. In catalogs, however, you may see it labeled *Delphinium ajacis*, which is an outdated scientific name.

Many gardeners have tried-and-true selections of larkspur in their gardens that reseed and return every year. Newer hybrids greatly expand the color palette. Rosamund is a soft rose; Los Angeles Improved is a salmon pink. Blue Spire Improved is a dark cool blue. Giant Imperial remains popular in mixes or with Imperial Blue Bell and Imperial White King. Blue Picotee is a pretty selection with white and lavender flowers. Among low-growing selections is Dwarf Hyacinth Flowered, a rich blue.

Troubleshooting

If you have trouble growing larkspur, your soil may be too acid. Add lime to raise the pH to 7, or neutral. You should also watch out for slugs; turn to page 124 to read about this pest.

A classic cottage-garden flower, larkspur is easy to grow and adds an air of nostalgia to beds and borders.

Lisianthus

Large, durable blooms and waxy, blue-gray foliage make for a striking garden display.

Tender-looking but tough, lisianthus is a newcomer to the garden scene. Much appreciated for its tolerance to heat and drought, it prefers poor soil and blooms all summer long in flower beds plagued with sandy soil. Lisianthus also thrives in containers.

Although native to Texas, lisianthus was brought to the attention of American gardeners by the Japanese, who hybridized it for the florist trade. The blooms last for weeks, and tall selections are excellent for cutting. Breeding has introduced dwarf versions of this flower for bedding. Fortunately, these newer versions retain the pioneer hardiness of wild lisianthus, also known as Texas Blue Bell.

A mass planting of lisianthus yields a sea of blue, white, or pink, or you can mix it with other annuals or perennials for spots of color. The plant has drought-resistant, waxy foliage that is bluish gray—a handsome companion to the colorful blooms.

AT A GLANCE
❖
LISIANTHUS
Eustoma grandiflorum

Features: large blooms, long flowering, drought tolerant
Colors: pink, white, blue
Height: 6 inches to 2 feet
Light: full sun
Soil: medium to dry, poor
Water: low to medium
Pests: none specific
Remarks: lasts for weeks as a cut flower

Flowering in profusion, lisianthus softens this formal hedge.

Planting and Care

Like so many plants that can take heat and drought, lisianthus does not like wet conditions. Well-drained soil is a must, making this a perfect annual for poor, sandy soil.

Set plants out in full sun after the last frost. While lisianthus needs little water and fertilizer, it does appreciate having its old blooms removed (which ensures continued blooming until the first fall frost). In areas seldom hit by frost, the foliage will remain all winter. In these locations, you may find that lisianthus acts as a perennial, sprouting again from dormant roots provided it has adequate drainage.

Lisianthus does not like acid soil. The pH of your soil should be nearly neutral, 6.5, for this annual to grow. To raise the pH, add lime to the soil in the pot or bed.

Different Selections

Lisianthus is seldom started from seed, so you are limited to the selections sold at local garden

Perfect for a terrace, potted lisianthus thrives during hot summer weather.

centers. Many of these are the dwarf types, such as Yodel, or the double-flowered selections, such as Echo, which grow about 2 feet tall and almost equally wide. Both need to be pinched as soon as you plant them to encourage a well-branched plant.

Newer selections, such as Blue Lisa, grow less than a foot tall; well branched and compact, they require no pinching. For cutting gardens, seek out the tallest selections, such as Heidi. Tall selections have blossoms concentrated at the top for greater show on longer stems.

Troubleshooting

It is essential to stake long-stemmed selections of lisianthus or they will be knocked down by storms. Tie them to a stake, or use a three-legged, grow-through support.

Madagascar Periwinkle

Many hybrid Madagascar periwinkle selections are prized for the size and clear color of their blooms.

If there is a bedding plant made for heat waves, it is Madagascar periwinkle. This rugged annual not only survives the scorching heat of July and August, it blooms right through it. In fact, it flowers from spring until the first fall frost. Even in drought, dependable Madagascar periwinkle brings summer color to garden borders, planters, and window boxes.

The blossoms of this hardy annual cover the glossy green mounds of foliage. They can be white, pink, rose, lavender, or, most recently, bright red—in solid colors or splashed at the center with a red, pink, or yellow starlet. Because of its low, spreading nature, Madagascar periwinkle should be planted where it will be easily seen, such as in the foreground of a flower border. The best effect comes from a mass planting; an area at least 10 feet square is recommended.

Should space be limited, tuck one or two plants in a location where the flowers can be enjoyed up close, such as along a garden path or beside steps. You should not refrain from planting it in containers to bring color to a deck, a terrace, or a patio. In Florida, Madagascar periwinkle grows like a wildflower, and because it is salt tolerant, it is a great plant for gardens near the beach.

Planting and Care

Unlike many annuals, Madagascar periwinkle does not respond well to a lot of water and fertilizer. It will languish in a garden during prolonged wet weather. These plants like poor, slightly dry soil. Either full sun or partial shade is fine, but flowering will be better in a sunny location.

In the spring, set out transplants rather than sowing seeds. This can be done about two weeks after the last frost. Never plant too early or periwinkle will rot, especially in a wet spring. Even plants set out

---

AT A GLANCE
❖

MADAGASCAR PERIWINKLE
Catharanthus roseus

Features: dependable summer color for hot, dry weather

Colors: white, pink, lavender, rose, red

Height: 3 to 20 inches

Light: full sun to partial shade

Soil: slightly dry, poor

Water: low, only when wilting after established

Pests: rot

Remarks: salt tolerant, great for the beach

later may be attacked by rot (fungus) if the weather is wet or there is a lot of dew. If rot becomes a problem, skip a year or two before planting Madagascar periwinkle again.

Water about once a week (count a good rain as a watering) for two to three weeks or until established. Then water only if the plants begin to wilt.

Different Selections

Madagascar periwinkle is generally classified in three groups, based on plant height: bush (also called standard), dwarf, and creeping (sometimes called extra dwarf). The bush types, such as the award-winning Parasol, grow 18 to 20 inches tall and provide a solid mass of color. The Pretty Series has captured attention with another award-winning plant, Pretty in Rose, which boasts large, mauve, velvety flowers with petals overlapping so that there are no gaps.

Catalogs describe the dwarf types as 8 to 10 inches tall; however, they may grow 11 to 14 inches tall in the South. Among dwarf selections are Little Blanche (white flowers), Little Bright Eye (white flowers with a red eye), Little Pinkie (rosy pink), and the Cooler series. Vinca Pacifica Red expands the periwinkle color palette to nearly red.

Creeping types reach a height of only 3 to 5 inches. These bloom only at the ends of the stems, so flower production is somewhat limited, but the plant works well for hanging baskets. Polka Dot is one selection of creeping Madagascar periwinkle.

Window boxes and other full-sun containers offer the perfect summer stage for Madagascar periwinkle.

Starting from Seed

For a fall encore of flowers, you can sow seeds of Madagascar periwinkle in August directly in the garden. Keep them well watered; flowering should begin in about three to four weeks. The plants will reseed, with subsequent blooms often reverting to pink shades. However, transplanting is recommended over seed sowing for the successful cultivation of Madagascar periwinkle.

Marigold

Pure sunset colors and fernlike foliage make marigolds a welcome addition to the summer and fall garden.

AT A GLANCE

❖

MARIGOLD
Tagetes hybrids

Features: brilliant sunset colors for summer and fall

Colors: yellow, orange, burnt red, burgundy, white

Height: 6 to 36 inches

Light: full sun

Soil: average

Water: medium

Pests: spider mites

Remarks: easy to grow from seed

Few garden flowers are more instantly recognizable than marigolds. These bright blossoms of burnt red, deep orange, bright yellow, creamy white, and bicolors have long been popular annuals for late spring and summer color. In the South, gardeners also set them out in late summer as an alternative to mums. Marigolds may be combined with other annuals and perennials in a flower bed or a pot, and they are popular as spots of color in vegetable gardens. Taller types can serve as filler in a perennial border or even as a background.

One of the easiest ways to use marigolds is in containers on a deck, a terrace, or a patio. Dwarf selections work well in strawberry jars and window boxes; they are also suited for the front of the flower border, as a low edging, and for tight planting areas in rock gardens.

Giant-flowered marigolds are popular for cutting, approaching zinnias in flower size. The tall types also work well as a bold flash of yellow or orange in a summer flower bed. Because the blooms are like giant medallions, a grouping of only three to five plants can make a good show.

Planting and Care

Marigolds need full sun to flower well and will grow best in fertile, moist, well-drained soil. They will also grow satisfactorily in poor soils, although they will not be as full. After danger of frost is past, sow seed directly in the ground or set out transplants. Transplants may grow slowly at first. The younger the plant, the better it will transplant. Space dwarf selections about 6 inches apart, and give taller selections about 12 inches.

Marigolds are moderately drought resistant, but will need water during extended dry periods. Dry weather also encourages spider mites. For best results, water marigolds every three or four rainless days, being sure to wet the foliage to discourage spider mites.

Keep plants blooming by pinching off faded flowers throughout the season; if spent blooms are not removed, flowering will decrease. Low-growing marigolds tend to become leggy by midsummer and blooms become sparse, especially in areas where night temperatures are high. The quickest and easiest way to rejuvenate these compact plants is to shear them back to about 6 inches high. Continue to trim them to keep them in bloom. Do not cut back taller types, as they will not do well when trimmed.

Different Selections

The many popular species of marigolds all originated in the Americas, despite the exotic names given to them by European growers. The African marigold *(Tagetes erecta)*, more recently called the American marigold, features large blossoms and leaves. The popular Dwarf French marigold *(Tagetes patula)* blooms early and bears smaller blooms than American marigolds. This plant yields good short-stemmed cut flowers and works well as a potted plant. Triploids, or "3-N" hybrids, are similar to Dwarf French types. They are compact, vigorous plants that are 12 to 16 inches in height and 14 to 20 inches across but bear larger blossoms than Dwarf French marigolds. The term **triploid** refers to an extra set of chromosomes that these plants have, usually resulting in larger blooms.

Signet marigolds *(Tagetes tenuifolia)* sport dainty single blossoms and are great for containers, edgings, and hanging baskets, as these plants do not have the stiff, erect form of other marigolds. Forming low-growing mats (8 to 12 inches in height) of lacy leaves and blossoms, signet marigolds may reach 2 feet or more in diameter. Available in yellow, orange, and gold, they look delightful in any container, especially strawberry jars. They are also slightly frost-tolerant, lasting longer into fall than other marigolds.

When buying transplants or seed, remember that marigolds are also grouped in garden centers by their landscape uses. Edging marigolds (10 inches or less in height) have short, neat forms that are good for outlining beds of taller flowers, bordering sidewalks, and filling containers. Series such as Boy, Janie, Little Devil, and Little Hero are typical of edging types. Spreading marigolds (8 to 12 inches in height), such as signet marigolds, provide a more free-form plant for containers and edgings.

Nothing beats marigolds for quick spots of color, as attested to by these dwarf selections in a strawberry jar.

Pom-pom flowers characterize the larger selections of marigolds.

Marigolds and chrysanthemums mixed with tall grasses create a fireworks of color and texture in the fall garden.

Divider marigolds (11 to 18 inches tall) are used in rows or drifts to divide groups of taller background plants and to provide a backdrop for low-growing edging flowers. Look for names such as Bonanza, Early Spice, Hero, Safari, Discovery, Inca, and Galore.

Background and tall marigolds (19 to 36 inches or more in height) are used in flower beds or accent groups, or to fill small beds, corners, and other small areas. They are also good for cutting, as their stems are long enough for use in arrangements. Series include Jubilee, Gold Coin, Climax, French Vanilla, and Snowdrift. Tall marigolds intended for cutting may require staking if you live in an area subject to heavy rain or windstorms.

Starting from Seed

Because they bloom quickly and are so easy to grow, marigolds are among the most popular flowers grown from seed. Scatter seed directly on top of the ground and pat so that it is in firm contact with the soil but never buried. If you choose to start seeds early indoors, sow in pots at least six weeks before the last frost.

Troubleshooting

Spider mites love marigold leaves and can be especially bad in dry weather. Check the underside of leaves before buying bedding plants to make sure that you are not bringing these pests home. See page 124 for more about spider mites.

In some areas of the South, the combination of long days and high temperatures can cause a temporary halt in blooming. Many gardeners work around both problems—halting blooms and spider mites—by planting a second crop of marigolds in late July or August.

Melampodium

Melampodium is a reliable staple of the summer garden. Lush yet drought tolerant, this annual is covered with 1-inch-wide, daisylike flowers and blooms without fail until frost. Planted in full sun or partial shade, it fills out with many branches like a small shrub, providing a bright mass of color that is ideal for flower beds and at the edge of wooded areas. It grows up to 18 inches tall and equally wide, with bright green foliage that adds almost as much to the color scheme as the flowers.

Use melampodium at the base of a mailbox or fence post; this plant does well in out-of-the-way places, as it can survive with little water. It can soften the abrupt corners of a low deck, steps, or the lines of walkways and raised beds. Because it stays neat and solid, it is ideal for borders and rock gardens. Melampodium's flowers are small but numerous and open just above the foliage, creating a nice contrast with larger flowers on long stems, such as daisies, coneflowers, or zinnias. Combine this annual with other yellows, such as lantana or marigold, or let it shine when paired with lilac verbena. It makes a good companion for sun-loving ferns, such as Southern Shield, because it can take a little shade. Melampodium also thrives in large tubs or planters on a deck or a patio.

Planting and Care

Melampodium is easy to grow. For blooms in early summer, set out transplants after the threat of frost is past. You may sow seed directly in the garden after the last frost, or in late spring for late summer and fall blooms.

Grow your own transplants indoors by sowing seeds two months prior to transplanting time. Water plants in lieu of rain until they are established, and then let nature take care of them. If the plants produce a lot of foliage and few blooms, plants may be getting too much shade or too much fertilizer. As for spent blooms, melampodium sheds them on its own, requiring no deadheading to continue blooming. Melampodium reseeds and will surprise you by springing up all over the garden to create new color combinations each summer.

Different Selections

Medallion is the most popular selection, growing 20 to 24 inches tall and boasting sunny golden blooms. In fact, melampodium is sometimes called medallion plant. In the wild, it is known as butter daisy.

A gently mounding plant, melampodium is a natural for edging pathways with sunny color and foliage that look good every day from spring until fall.

AT A GLANCE

❖

MELAMPODIUM
Melampodium paludosum

Features: mounding annual with bright green leaves and yellow blooms

Colors: golden yellow

Height: 18 to 24 inches

Light: full sun to very light shade

Soil: well drained

Water: medium

Pests: none specific

Remarks: foliage is as attractive as blooms

Mexican Mint Marigold

These single blooms have a simple, old-fashioned quality.

Although planted in spring, this annual does not bloom until the fall. However, gardeners can enjoy the feathery green foliage of Mexican mint marigold in the meantime. Established plants bear an occasional flower in the spring but bloom profusely in the fall. When the plant finally blooms, flowers top 1- to 2-foot-tall stems.

The feathery foliage of Mexican mint marigold resembles that of the culinary herb French tarragon, which does not grow in hot, humid climates. Herb gardeners across the South have discovered that this heat-tolerant, anise-scented plant can be substituted in recipes that need the flavor of tarragon. You can snip fresh sprigs as needed, beginning in spring. Or simply enjoy the color and form of this handsome herb. Known as mint marigold in Texas, this annual is called Mexican tarragon by Floridians, and sweet-scented marigold or Spanish tarragon by others.

Combine Mexican mint marigold with chrysanthemums in a flower bed, or let it be a bright spot in your herb garden, which often looks tired by summer's end. Although grown as an annual in most of the country, Mexican mint marigold behaves as a half-hardy perennial in warmer regions. With regular, light frosts in the Lower South, it dies above ground, but if mulched, the roots will survive overnight dips as low as 5 degrees. In the southern tips of Florida and Texas, it never dies down.

Planting and Care

Mexican mint marigold is available as seeds or transplants. It will grow in full sun or partial shade, but demands well-drained soil. Once established, it spreads from stems that root when they fall to the ground; propagate young plants to bring indoors for winter by rooting stems. In areas with hard winters, plant in the spring. However, transplants set in Coastal South gardens in the fall will develop root systems during the winter and grow vigorously in spring.

The yellow flowers of Mexican mint marigold are a showy addition to fall flower gardens.

Morning Glory and Moonflower

Morning glories provide quick summer color for fences, porches, or trellises.

Two closely related vines, morning glory *(Ipomoea purpurea)* and moonflower *(Ipomoea alba)*, refresh the garden with their lush, heart-shaped foliage and broad, saucerlike flowers from early summer until the first frost. Given full sun and regular watering, these vigorous vines thrive in heat, growing a foot or more per week, to stretch across a handrail or a fence in little time. Few plants reward the gardener with better value, as one packet of seeds is enough to envelop an entire garden in glorious lengths of blooming vine.

Morning glory and moonflower make a great pair. Morning glory blooms in the morning, with its delicate blossoms closing by midday. A few hours later, the fragrant moonflower opens its lovely white blooms and perfumes the air. Plant them around any vertical structure: the post of a mailbox, a fence, an arbor, or the supports of a porch or a deck. They will grow in large pots if given frequent water and something to climb. Because they grow quickly and live only one season, these vines can be planted where a more slow-growing perennial will eventually be, filling an otherwise blank space.

Morning Glory

Morning glory vines twine to lengths of 8 to 10 feet or more, providing profuse and continuous flowers in shades of blue, pink, lavender, or crimson. Although the blooms are only open to greet you in the morning, the plant itself is wonderfully rugged, thriving in heavy clay or poor sand along roadsides all over the country. It will twine and climb a support, or sprawl as a ground cover where there is nothing to climb. You can also create lovely combinations, pairing morning glory with other vines, such as the tropical mandevilla or fall-blooming clematis.

Moonflower

This vine could be called evening glory, as it comes to life when the sun sets. Its large, saucer-shaped blooms unfurl quickly, often in less than a minute, in late afternoon. They are a treat for anyone, especially children. Aptly named, moonflower's broad blooms reflect moonlight, making it a great choice for planting around patios and decks where you spend time on summer evenings. The blooms are also sweetly fragrant and attract large sphinx moths that flutter like hummingbirds. Moonflower is very vigorous, growing 10 to 15 feet or more; this vine is capable of overtaking nearby plants, so it is best used alone or combined with vines that are equally vigorous.

Planting and Care

Morning glory and moonflower grow best when started from seed sown directly in the garden. Plant in full sun after all danger of frost has passed. Nick the hard coat of the seeds with a nail file and soak in a pan of water for several hours. Morning glory and moonflower are not picky about their soil, growing in rich or poor ground. Water plants until they are well established. After that, they are drought tolerant, but the leaves will temporarily wilt at the height of a scorching summer day.

If you want to plant these vines along a fence, plant two seeds (inches apart) every 4 to 5 feet and train young vines in opposite directions. The vines are likely to grow out of hand in a small-scale planting, such as around a mailbox, so be prepared to cut them back. Otherwise, give them a sturdy support with plenty of room to roam. They will grow and twist up a small trellis, but you will need to use twine or other supports to keep the vines on lampposts, columns, or other large, smooth structures. Both morning glory and moonflower will bloom longer if you deadhead old blooms to keep seed pods from forming.

Different Selections

For morning glory, Heavenly Blue remains one of the most popular selections, with its sky blue color fading to white toward the center of 5-inch-wide flowers. Sunrise Mixed features an array of striped and bicolored flowers in pink, purple, rose, lilac, sky blue, and white. Scarlett O'Hara is an All-America Selections winner with rich crimson flowers. Tall Mixed contains a range of colors and climbs higher than other selections. Crimson Rambler produces deep magenta flowers that are attractive to hummingbirds.

There are few named selections of moonflower. Giant White is one selection frequently found in seed catalogs. All moonflowers boast fragrant, white flowers that may be 6 inches across.

At a Glance
❖
MOONFLOWER
Ipomoea alba

Features: summer vine that blooms at night
Colors: white
Height: 10 to 15 feet
Light: full sun
Soil: rich to poor and sandy
Water: medium
Pests: none specific
Remarks: fast growing, fragrant

Moonflower unfurls quickly in late afternoon; plant it where you can enjoy its sweet fragrance.

Moss Rose and Purslane

The pure, bright flowers of purslane bask in the sun but stay closed on cloudy days.

Moss rose and purslane earn their keep in the heat of summer. Both plants have drought-tolerant, succulent leaves and do not grow or bloom well until the weather warms up in late spring. Old-fashioned moss rose bears delicate, roselike blossoms in soft shades of orange, red, yellow, pink, and white. Its succulent leaves are gray green and needlelike, and the plants spread up to 2 feet wide and 4 to 6 inches tall. Moss rose is good for beds, rock gardens, rock walls, and containers, but its stems are too brittle for hanging baskets.

Moss rose is named for the roselike fullness of its blooms.

Purslane is a hybrid that is often sold in hanging baskets. It has single flowers and spoon-shaped leaves on trailing stems. (This is not the same plant as the weedy, yellow-flowered purslane that invades lawns and pastures.)

Because of their succulent leaves and stems, moss rose and purslane are nearly as tolerant of summer heat as cacti. They like to bask in the sun, opening their flowers in the morning and closing them in the heat of the afternoon. On extremely hot days, the blooms may close by noon, especially if the soil is dry. On cloudy days, flowers are slow to open or may remain closed.

Both moss rose and purslane may be used anywhere a low-growing, creeping flower will do—edgings, beds, rock gardens, dry banks, between paving stones. Because of their brightly colored blossoms, they make a great summer ground cover. Their tolerance of drought makes them good choices for containers, too.

Purslane makes a great summer container plant.

AT A GLANCE

❖

MOSS ROSE AND PURSLANE

Portulaca species and hybrids

Features: creeping, drought-tolerant mat with colorful summer blooms

Colors: yellow, white, pink, red, purple, salmon

Height: 4 to 8 inches

Light: full sun

Soil: well drained; average, rocky, or sandy

Water: low

Pests: none specific

Remarks: tolerates sun and poor soil

Planting and Care

Well-drained soil is a must. These plants do well in sandy soil and are great for gardens near the beach. After the danger of frost has passed, moss rose can be started from transplants, but it sprouts easily from seed, too. Purslane is sold as transplants or as established plants in hanging baskets. It is grown only from cuttings, either commercially propagated in a greenhouse or from a plant which you have saved; seed is not available.

Although they are very drought tolerant, young plants should be watered and fertilized to encourage quick growth. Cut plants back by about one-third if they creep out of bounds. Keep baskets of purslane full in the center by cutting a few of the branches back every month. Snipping off old blooms will keep the plants blooming until the first cold snap.

Purslane forms a dense, colorful summer ground cover.

Different Selections

Moss rose selections include the Sundial series, one of the first to allow you to choose one specific color. (Most selections are sold as a multicolored mix.) Minilaca is named for its extremely compact 2-inch plants that stay short and do not spread. Purslane is rarely sold by selection name but rather by color; as seed is not available, you will not find it listed in seed catalogs.

Starting from Seed

Moss rose (not purslane) is easy to start from seed. Sow after the last frost. The seeds are tiny; just scatter them in the soil, between stones, or wherever you would like a blooming ground cover. Keep seeds watered until plants germinate and become established. It will be two months before blooms appear.

Moss rose spills its blooms into a walkway.

Pansy, Viola, and Johnny-Jump-Up

Yellow pansies make blues and purples appear brighter.

Pansy, viola, and Johnny-jump-up are related flowers that are prized for fall, winter, and spring color. Botanically, all are *Viola* species, and each will delight you with a variety of colors and uses. Although all are low growing, the main difference between the three is the size of the leaves and the blooms, which allows you to fine-tune their uses in the landscape.

In the South, few bedding plants can hold their own against the changing seasons like these do. Plant a group in the fall, and they will bloom right away. Give them light mulch for protection, and they will bloom in winter, with each warm spell bringing out a splash of color. By spring, they are finally free to bloom like never before. Plants will be covered in flowers throughout March and April before fading in the heat.

Pansy

Pansies *(Viola x Wittrockiana)* boast the largest plants and blooms of this group, but they are still rather low, generally growing only 6 to 10 inches tall. Because they are low growing, pansies are ideal for planting in the front of a border or in a bed beside a terrace or walk. If they become lanky and flop or spill from their beds, you can trim them back a few inches. They are also striking when massed in a single color in formal beds.

Pansies are great companions for other flowers, especially early spring bulbs, such as daffodils and tulips. Through winter, pansies

bring color that is close to the ground, and in spring, the bulbs will provide another level of colorful blooms above. Pansies also make lovely companions for iris, filling out the bed in winter. A row of tall pastel foxgloves behind a solid row of blue pansies can make an elegant impression. They also mingle well with ivy in containers. And, some pansies have a delicate perfume that adds a slight fragrance in addition to charming color.

When the weather turns cold, do not be concerned that pansies will fade; many selections can tolerate temperatures as low as 15 degrees.

Viola

Violas *(Viola cornuta)* are often called minipansies because they look so much like small pansies. The smaller scale of their leaves, stems, and flowers makes them perfect for pots from fall through spring. Violas seldom flop over like pansies and are perfect for pots in combination with spring bulbs. The smaller size of these blooms is reminiscent of violets.

Johnny-Jump-Up

The smallest of the group, Johnny-jump-up *(Viola tricolor)*, is also known as Good King Henry. Plant in fall to enjoy early spring flowers. They prefer partial shade and rich, well-drained soil. They often reseed, so they will return each year. Plant Johnny-jump-ups in a quiet spot near steps, an entryway, or on the edge of a wooded garden. They like to reseed between stones, in gravel, or between cracks in pavement. Colors range from white and lemon yellow to violet blue and tricolored of violet, lavender, and yellow.

Different Selections

Pansies come in three different classifications based largely on size of bloom: large (3½ to 4½ inches), medium (2½ to 3½ inches), and multiflora (1½ to 2½ inches). Among large pansies are Swiss Giant, Accord, and Majestic Giant series; because of their size, they are also popular as cut flowers. Medium-sized pansies include Crown (all solid colors), Joker, Roc, and Imperial series, perfect for pots or bedding. The Imperial series is prized for its vigorous growth and unique shades, particularly pink. Multiflora types are also called landscape

Joker Light Blue vibrates with color.

A white pansy mixes well with all colors and looks lovely at night.

Imperial Orange Prince, an All-America Selections winner, is noted for its unique color.

The front of a tulip border is an ideal place for pansies.

Violas offer smaller, more delicate blooms than pansies.

pansies because they are so profuse for bedding. Although the blossoms are smaller than those of other pansies, they produce so many blooms that it is difficult to see their foliage. They are more heat tolerant, lasting until the final days of spring. Noteworthy selections include Universal, Maxim, and Crystal Bowl series and Padparadja, an unusual orange.

Violas are available in all the same colors as pansies. Some have a white throat or a yellow eye in the center of the flower. The Jewel and Princess series offer 1-inch blooms in yellow, white, and shades of purple.

AT A GLANCE

❖
VIOLA
Viola cornuta

Features: small pansylike blooms

Colors: white, violet, lavender, yellow

Height: 7 inches

Light: full sun

Soil: rich, well drained

Water: medium

Pests: slugs

Remarks: great for pots

The deep yellow blossoms of Universal Hybrid pansies bring out the yellow centers of Shasta daisies.

The Alpine Summer series of Johnny-jump-up features tricolored blooms of yellow, light blue, and dark blue. Blue Elf has flowers of violet blue, and Helen Mount combines violet, lavender, and yellow in a single bloom.

Planting and Care

Fall is the time to plant pansies, violas, and Johnny-jump-ups in the South; they will grow to twice the size and produce more flowers than those planted in the spring. Spring-planted pansies do not have time to become well established before they start blooming. Colder climates call for spring planting, but pansies will last much later into the summer than they do in the South because of the cooler nights.

Plants need at least six hours of sun; plants in shade will produce fewer blooms. Set transplants 6 to 8 inches apart, and water regularly when the weather is dry. In late winter, reapply a slow-release flower food (see page 28). Be sure to keep the plants watered; although forgiving and quick to spring back from wilting, plants will bloom better if the soil is kept moist. As the weather gets hot in the summer, flowers get smaller and plants look weak and stressed. Replace them with annuals that can beat the heat.

Troubleshooting

Slugs often attack the succulent growth of these plants, chewing holes in both the flowers and the foliage. Turn to page 124 for more information about slugs.

Johnny-jump-ups will reseed and spring back again every year.

AT A GLANCE
❖
JOHNNY-JUMP-UP
Viola tricolor

Features: early spring flowers that are smaller than pansies
Colors: blue, tricolored (violet, lavender, yellow)
Height: 7 inches
Light: partial shade
Soil: rich, well drained
Water: medium
Pests: slugs
Remarks: will reseed

Pots of yellow pansies are glowing spots of color. Planted in the fall, they will overwinter in pots in warmer zones.

Petunia

Petunias can be solid or bicolored.

Unlike most annuals, which are either cool- or warm-weather plants, petunias are a little bit of both. Although you see them sold mostly in spring for summer bedding, they are actually great annuals for fall or even winter in the Coastal and Lower South.

You can mix petunias with other plants in flower beds, mass them for a sea of color, or use them as cascading accents in a mixed pot of annuals. Spreading types also make a unique seasonal ground cover. Pastel and white petunias are especially nice in the evening because their large, disklike blooms reflect moonlight and night lighting.

Planting and Care

The best way to start petunias is from transplants set out in early spring, or in late summer for a fall show. Plant in full sun and in well-drained soil. Petunias do well in poor, sandy soil and will tolerate heavy clay and alkaline soil as long as it is well drained.

In the Lower and Coastal South, you may plant petunias in fall for blooms through three seasons. Choose a selection that is heat tolerant and keep the plants well tended to see blooms from winter until the following summer. Many selections will tolerate light frost with no damage; if you live beyond coastal areas, you should experiment to see how long a fall planting will bloom before being killed by a hard freeze. In the Upper and Middle South, plant petunias in spring after the last frost for blooms until the first hard freeze.

To keep plants lush and blooming profusely, trim them back an inch or two when they reach 6 inches tall. Transplants are often this tall when purchased; if so, pinch them at planting time. As the plants grow, continue pinching off old blooms to encourage more blooms and branching. You will need to feed the plants again with slow-release plant food in mid- to late summer. If the plants have grown leggy by midsummer, prune them back to about one-half their height and water and fertilize as if they were newly planted. This will encourage a new flush of both foliage and flowers for spring.

Different Selections

You will find subtle variety among petunia selections, each with its own strengths. A few selections are fragrant, often releasing their perfume at night to attract moths, which then pollinate the flowers. Many petunias have double, frilled blooms; some are more heat tolerant than others. Choose a selection that suits your garden's needs.

Grandiflora petunias grow about 8 inches tall and produce the largest blooms, 4 to 5 inches in diameter. These are very showy in pots and baskets. However, they are the most likely to be battered by rain and they do not like hot weather. In the South, consider these only for fall or early spring. Grandiflora types include deeply ruffled blooms, such as Can Can, and double blooms, such as Purple Pirouette. Double petunias need extra fertilizer to develop their extra-large blossoms; feed them with a liquid food every third watering.

Multiflora petunias grow about 8 inches tall and have smaller blooms than grandiflora petunias, but more of them. They are more tolerant of hot weather than the giant-flowered grandiflora types. Multiflora petunias will last through summer even in the South if trimmed back and watered and fertilized properly. Primetime is a popular Multiflora series. These plants stay fairly compact even in the hot South. Colors include pink, red, salmon, blue, and white.

Floribunda petunias also have good tolerance to heat. Proven series include Madness, which will survive summer in the South if trimmed back and kept watered and fertilized. The Madness series is available in the standard range of petunia colors and includes double-flowered types. Another proven series is Celebrity, which includes 2- to 3-inch blooms of white and shades of pink, purple, and red.

Double-flowered petunias are more finicky than single blooms but are nonetheless popular for their unusual fullness. This one is Purple Pirouette.

Cascading petunias are ground-hugging plants that grow only 4 to 6 inches tall but may be 36 inches wide. Cascading petunias, such as Supertunia, Cascadia, and Purple Wave, are popular for hanging baskets and as a seasonal ground cover.

Seeds and seedlings of old-fashioned single types, many without names, are often passed among gardeners. These 12- to 18-inch-tall plants are very rugged, establishing themselves in one place and reappearing year after year, even in sandy soil. They bear single blooms in shades of pink and lavender.

The floppy stems of petunias make these annuals perfect for low window boxes, where they can be easily watered, trimmed, and fertilized for a long-lasting show.

Single, old-fashioned petunias are among the most rugged selections and will often reseed themselves.

Poppy

Shirley poppies bloom in an array of colors with interesting markings.

Though fragile in appearance, poppies are quite tough plants whose tufts of foliage are not bothered by cold and whose flowers dance in a spring breeze. Whether massed for solid color or mixed with other annuals and perennials, they animate beds and borders with their paperlike petals in both soft and bright colors. There are several species of annual poppies, but all share the same graceful flowers and similar appearance; once started in a garden, all keep themselves going by reseeding year after year.

Shirley Poppy

The annual Shirley poppy blooms in bright colors atop lanky stems that grow to 3 feet tall. These flowers have yellow or white centers with pink, rose, scarlet, or salmon petals. You can also find bicolored and double-flowered forms. And like their wild relatives, which were brought back by World War I soldiers from Flanders in northwest Europe, Shirley poppies develop strong plants wherever their seeds fall. They will reseed from one year to the next in soil that is left uncultivated and free of mulch.

To grow Shirley poppies, you may set out transplants in spring, but it is easier to sow seeds directly into the garden in early fall or late winter. If planted in fall, plants will sprout but will stay small through winter and then begin to grow as the weather gets warmer in spring.

AT A GLANCE

❖

SHIRLEY POPPY
Papaver rhoeas

Features: showy blooms for beds, borders, and bouquets

Colors: white, pink, lilac, orange, yellow, red

Height: 12 to 36 inches

Light: full sun

Soil: average, well drained

Water: medium

Pests: none specific

Remarks: reseeds easily

Because of their thin, wispy stems, Shirley poppies look best when planted in large masses.

Iceland Poppy

Another poppy you can sow directly in the garden in fall is Iceland poppy, *Papaver nudicaule*. Although it is biennial, Iceland poppy will sometimes behave like a perennial when planted in cool regions. It dies down after blooming in spring and then resumes growth in the fall. The foliage is hardy enough to remain green during the mild winters of the South, making Iceland poppy a great annual to plant in fall. It will bloom in spring, but it will not survive the hot, humid summer.

Unlike other poppies, Iceland poppies do not have leaves on their stems, which makes them terrific for use in arrangements of cut flowers. Cut them in the morning just as their blooms open. The flowers will continue to develop once in water. Before arranging cut poppies with other flowers, you will need to sear the ends of the stems with a flame or plunge them into boiling water for about 20 seconds to stop the leakage of white sap. Then place them in deep water for a minimum of four hours to get them in good condition for arranging.

Iceland poppies come in a variety of colors, including this bright, sunny yellow.

AT A GLANCE

❖

CALIFORNIA POPPY
Eschscholzia californica

Features: showy blooms for beds, borders, and bouquets

Colors: white, pink, orange, yellow, red

Height: 12 to 36 inches

Light: full sun

Soil: alkaline, well drained

Water: low to medium

Pests: none specific

Remarks: needs alkaline soil

California Poppy

California poppies *(Eschscholzia californica)* are known for their soft, breeze-blown flowers that look beautiful when planted in masses to mimic their presence in the wild. This poppy is native to the West and prefers alkaline soil, making it a good choice for Texas and other areas where the soil pH is high.

Although perennial in its home state, California poppy is grown as an annual in the South. Sow seeds in fall, as they need cool weather to germinate. California poppies also need a lot of water to sprout. If the seed bed dries during the critical two to three week germination period, the seeds will not sprout. If you do not have alkaline soil, add lime to the soil a few weeks before planting to raise the soil pH to 7 or more.

Opium Poppy

Long-time gardeners may know opium poppy, *Papaver somniferum,* quite well. It is one of the best poppies for the South and is often found in old gardens. Opium poppy is prized for its blooms, which may be various shades of pink or white; some types have double blooms and are called peony flowered; double poppies with fringed petals are referred to as carnation flowered. In addition to its handsome blooms, this poppy also has beautiful waxy blue foliage and is one of the most heat tolerant of all poppies, lasting into late spring and early summer.

Different Selections

One of the available selections of Shirley poppy, Mother of Pearl, offers delicate shades of soft blue, lilac, pink, white, and peach on plants that grow about 3 feet tall. All-Double Shirley bears double flowers on 2-foot plants in white, rose, salmon, and red.

Among Iceland poppies, Champagne Bubbles provides a good mix of solids and some bicolored blooms on full plants, about 1 foot tall. Wonderland is another low-growing selection (12 to 14 inches) that works well as a bedding plant. It has large flowers on short, sturdy stems.

California poppies are known for their natural orange hue, but breeders have developed selections that include yellow, red, pinks, and white. Ballerina Mixed boasts flowers up to 3 inches wide on 1-foot-tall plants.

The thin petals of poppies are nearly translucent. Here they glow among purple and pink bachelor's buttons in a field of color.

Although opium poppy is an heirloom and seeds are often passed among gardeners with no reference to an official and lasting name, there are a few selections listed in seed catalogs. Peony-Flowered Oase is named for its fringed double blooms of bright scarlet that resemble peonies. White Cloud bears extra-double white blooms. Hens and Chicks is grown for its sturdy, extra-large seed pods for use in crafts.

Planting and Care

All of the poppies described here may be started from seed directly in the garden in fall or late winter in the South, and in early spring in areas with colder winters. All need full sun, and soil with excellent drainage is a must; otherwise, the plants will rot in winter.

The seeds are small (like the poppy seeds sprinkled on foods). If you mix them with a little sand before you sow, or put them in an old kitchen poppy-seed container and use it as a dispenser, you can sprinkle seeds evenly over the area. Let the seeds sit on top of the ground and keep them moist with daily waterings.

Although poppies resent transplanting, you can grow them in containers to be planted in the garden if you transplant while the seedlings are very young (about 1 or 2 inches in diameter). Set transplants 8 to 10 inches apart. Even poppies that reseed themselves need thinning or the plants may be so crowded that their stems will grow weak and may be knocked down by hard rain.

Double-flowered selections wear their petals like a skirt of many layers.

AT A GLANCE
❖
OPIUM POPPY
Papaver somniferum

Features: showy spring blooms for beds and borders
Colors: white, pink
Height: 36 inches
Light: full sun
Soil: average, well drained
Water: medium
Pests: none specific
Remarks: reseeds easily

Poppy buds are nearly as attractive as the full blooms.

Rose Verbena

Drought-tolerant rose verbena is forgiving should you forget to water, making it a good choice for containers.

Rose verbena shakes off heat and humidity, welcoming summer and spreading like a ground cover in even the most sultry climates. A Southern native, rose verbena is a low-growing, creeping plant that is covered from midspring to fall in clusters of tiny, velvety pink, white, or purple flowers and finely-cut, dark leaves.

Ranging from 6 to 24 inches tall, rose verbena has a niche in summer in flower beds and borders, especially those in full sun. Its open, branching foliage permits other plants to grow up around and through it. Rose verbena works well when planted with bulbs, disguising their leaves as they fade. Plant purple selections behind yellow marigolds, coreopsis, or coneflowers around a mailbox or in a perennial border. Or allow it to creep onto the edge of a walkway, add color and texture to a rock garden, or perk up a container of less vivid plants.

Rose verbena softly spills over this wall as it would over a rocky bank in the wild.

Mix rose verbena with yellow lantana or pink petunias in a window box or hanging basket to attract hummingbirds and butterflies. Plant it with Lance Whorton caladiums, which can take more sun than most caladiums, or with any other sun lover to bring a reliable touch of color to the sunniest areas of your garden.

Planting and Care

Set out transplants in full sun after all danger of frost has passed. Rose verbena enjoys well-drained garden soil and does very well in poor, sandy soil. Set plants 20 to 24 inches apart, as they will quickly form a wavy, loose-knit carpet of flowers. Remove faded flowers to encourage fresh blooms; plants may also need to be cut back during the summer when they become leggy.

Rose verbena may be grown as a short-lived perennial in the Lower and Coastal South and warmer portions of the Middle South. Elsewhere, it is a warm-weather annual, thriving from late spring until the first frost.

Different Selections

The lightly fragrant Homestead Purple sports rich purple blooms and grassy green foliage and is an excellent performer. Abbeville has fragrant, lavender blooms.

While not as hardy as its native cousin, trailing verbena also functions well in summer baskets and in edgings, and features several named selections, including Imagination, with deep violet spring-to-fall flowers, and Sissinghurst, with rose-pink blooms.

Troubleshooting

Spider mites and whiteflies love verbena. Although the plants are tough enough to endure infestations without pesticide, the foliage of plants under attack will be mottled and lose its dark green sheen. Turn to page 124 for more about these pests.

Rose verbena may be found in several shades of pink and purple.

Scarlet Sage

When planted in a mass under the light shade of pines, scarlet sage looks like wildflowers.

Scarlet sage is one-of-a-kind for summer. Its flower spikes are strong and vertical and combine well with plants that have flat, round flowers and a mounding or horizontal form. Because its drama can overpower other flowers, be sure to pair it with something that can match its energy. Yellow marigolds and red or purple scarlet sage can be combined vividly from late spring until the first frost. Used with a silver-leafed plant, such as dusty miller or artemisia, its red stands alone. White flowers, such as petunias or impatiens, are a nice foil to the brilliance of scarlet sage.

Scarlet sage is also effective when planted in a bold, solid mass. You will need to plant a group of at least a dozen plants to create a dense sweep of color. In a naturalistic landscape, the open-flowering habit of the individual plants can be used to its best advantage. Plant small groups of scarlet sage beneath pines for a colorful effect that is reminiscent of wildflowers. Compact selections are suitable for containers, too.

Planting and Care

Set out transplants of scarlet sage in spring, after the danger of frost has passed. Red selections do well in either full sun or partial shade, but white, purple, and rose selections may scorch in the sun. These definitely need partial shade. All selections of scarlet sage like fertile, well-drained soil. Water regularly during periods of dry weather as the plants will not flower without it. Snip off old flower spikes as they fade to keep the plants compact and to encourage continued flowering until frost. To promote compact, multi-branched plants, pinch transplants as soon as you set them out.

Different Selections

Despite the name, not all selections of scarlet sage are red. White, rose, salmon, and purple selections are also available. Selections range from 8 inches to more than 30 inches tall, with the low-growing ones flowering earliest in the season and the tallest

Although called scarlet sage, this annual can be found in shades other than red.

beginning about a month later. Use low-growing selections (8 to 12 inches tall), such as Flamenco and Red Hot Sally, at the edge of a border or in a small pot. Plants growing from 14 to 20 inches include Top Burgundy and Blaze of Fire. The tallest ones grow to 24 to 30 inches and include Bonfire, America, and Splendens Tall. In the South, plants may grow 4 to 6 inches taller than the label states, especially in the shade.

You will see two similar plants, *Salvia coccinea* and *Salvia elegans* (pineapple sage), for sale in garden centers and catalogs. Although perennial in the Lower and Coastal South, they are annual in the rest of the country. Lady in Red is the most popular selection of *Salvia coccinea*, growing to about 3 feet tall and equally wide. Pineapple sage is sold as an herb because of its scented foliage. Both of these annuals attract hummingbirds.

The red blooms of pineapple sage are smaller than those of scarlet sage.

Scarlet sage is one of the summer's showiest annuals. Here, a salmon selection continues into fall in combination with wild ageratum, salvia, goldenrod, and chrysanthemums.

Snapdragon

Tall, colorful snapdragons make great back-of-the-border plants when contrasted with lower flowers, such as petunias.

AT A GLANCE
❖
SNAPDRAGON
Antirrhinum majus

Features: old-fashioned favorite that blooms during the cool season

Colors: yellow, white, pink, red, maroon, orange, bronze, bicolored

Height: 6 to 36 inches

Light: full sun to very light shade

Soil: fertile, well drained, neutral

Water: medium

Pests: none specific

Remarks: tall selections make great cut flowers

Along with their ice-cream colors and frilly flowers, snapdragons are treasured for their strong vertical lines in a flower bed. Snapdragons, or snaps, as they are often called, like cool weather and bring dependable color from winter through spring in the Lower and Coastal South. Farther north, they come alive in spring and summer gardens as spikes of vivid color. They contrast beautifully with other flowers, especially those that hold their blooms horizontally, such as Shasta daisies.

You can mass snapdragons in waves for a solid watercolored effect, plant tall ones as a backdrop at the back of the border, or vary them with lower mounding plants. They also mix well with other colors, as in the marriage of bright yellow snaps and Shasta daisies, or pastel snaps and soft shades of pansies. Dwarf snaps are low-mounding plants that are excellent as edging, fillers in perennial beds, or accents in containers. Taller snaps make excellent cut flowers, lasting a week or more in a vase.

Snapdragons are also fun for children, who can pull down the lower half of the bloom to reveal its mouthlike center. When let go, the flower snaps shut, hence the name.

Planting and Care

In the Coastal and Lower South, and warmer parts of the Middle South, set out young transplants in the fall to give them time to establish themselves before cold weather hits. In cooler areas, set out transplants in early spring.

Snaps like fertile, well-drained soil in full sun but will tolerate light shade, though they will flower less profusely. Water during periods of dry weather or the plants will not grow to their full size and flower height.

With the exception of dwarf types, each plant will first form a tall flower spike in the center. When this initial spike fades, cut it off at the base and smaller side spikes will appear. Snaps will stop blooming if their flowers, which form seed, are not removed. You can also encourage plants to form more spikes from the beginning by pinching the tops off young transplants when you first set them out; these secondary spikes will be smaller than the first.

Taller types, which are popular for cutting, need to be staked with a grow-through support, stick, or tomato cage. In the South, snaps bloom about a month longer than pansies in the summer before they need to be pulled up. Keep them blooming as long as possible by pinching old blooms and watering regularly.

Snapdragons can be grown from seed, but the seed is very small and hard to sow. Transplants also need nearly four months to grow from seed until flowering starts, and it is hard to keep them cool enough in summer to be ready for fall planting. Snaps grow best when started from transplants.

Different Selections

Snapdragons come in three heights, each suited to a particular garden use. Colors may be vivid or pastel and range from white, yellow, and orange to rose, red, bronze, and bicolored. Dwarf selections, such as Tahiti and Pixie, grow 6 to 15 inches tall to provide mounds of color.

Medium to tall selections grow 16 to 30 inches in height and include Liberty, Madame Butterfly, Princess, and Sonnet. Often these form secondary side spikes that flower after the central, taller spike, thereby extending the length of blooming time and the fullness of the plant.

The tallest snapdragons grow from 24 to 36 inches high and include Bright Butterflies, Panorama, and Rocket. All are prized for cutting and for their strikingly colorful, vertical spikes in beds and, particularly, borders.

Snapdragons offer a full range of color, from bright yellows, reds, and oranges to pastel pinks and pure white.

Snow-on-the-Mountain

Snow-on-the-mountain leaves are gray green with white variegation.

The gray-green leaves of snow-on-the-mountain are rimmed with white, as if tipped with frost. However, they are merely a cool illusion during the blistering summer. When some annuals suffer in the heat of summer, along comes snow-on-the-mountain, a tenacious, reseeding annual that grows wild from the Dakotas to Texas and thrives in full sun or partial shade, in any soil.

This annual, grown for its reliable, variegated foliage, adds stability to a perennial bed as the other plants wax and wane. Its showy green-and-white leaves also help blend the colors of neighboring plants and tone down nearby bright blooms. For a lovely, old-fashioned effect, combine snow-on-the-mountain with spider flower. Although the foliage has the greatest visual impact, you will find dainty white flowers at the tip of each branch. Later these flowers will be replaced by a cluster of round pods that hold the promise of snow-on-the-mountain next spring.

Planting and Care

You can plant snow-on-the-mountain any time between the last spring frost and midsummer. Choose a sunny, well-drained location, and sow the seed directly into the garden soil as this annual is difficult to transplant. When seedlings emerge, they will not be variegated like the mature plant but will be gray green in color. Thin seedlings to 12 to 18 inches apart. After the seedlings begin to branch out, the variegation will appear.

Snow-on-the-mountain has a milky sap like that of its relative, poinsettia. The foliage is lovely in arrangements of summer flowers, but the cut ends of the stems must be seared in a flame to stop the sap from running. If you have sensitive skin, be careful when handling the stems; the sap can be irritating.

Different Selections

Although snow-on-the-mountain will generally grow to a height of about 3 feet, a selection called Summer Icicle is only 18 inches tall.

Troubleshooting

Once you plant snow-on-the-mountain, you must be willing to pull up unwanted seedlings. This annual will reappear at will throughout your garden. Be prepared to pull volunteer seedlings each year; if you wish to share seedlings with friends, transplant while the plants are young and have only two to four leaves.

Spider Flower

This tall and airy annual, sometimes called cleome, shrugs off heat and drought and blooms from early summer until the first killing frost. By summer's end, each plant may stand 5 feet tall and sport a half dozen spreading stalks that wave in even the slightest breeze. Because of its tall stalks and large leaves, spider flower tends to dwarf its own airy blossoms of white, pink, or lavender. You can grow spider flower as an annual hedge or plant it at the rear of a mixed border. It also looks great in a carefree cottage garden or in front of a picket fence.

Spider flower is one of the best annuals for flower arrangements because of its unusual blooms with long, whiskerlike stamens that resemble spider legs. The petals curl up during the hotter part of the day and then slowly unfurl in the cooler evening. The best time to cut new blossoms is in late afternoon and evening when spider flower springs to life. Its long, coiled stamens burst forth, popping open the day's new flowers.

Planting and Care

The easiest way to start spider flower is to sow seed directly in the garden in early spring, about two weeks before the last frost. Space the plants 3 feet apart. If planted too close together, plants will be thin and scrawny. Because transplants will outgrow their tiny pots quickly, they are often hard to find in a nursery. If you should find them, wait until after the last frost to plant.

For best effect in the landscape, plant spider flower in large masses. Select a site in full sun with well-drained soil. Once established, spider flower tolerates dry weather, but the lower leaves will turn yellow and the flowers will wilt quickly if the plant needs water.

Starting from Seed

To grow your own transplants, start seed four to six weeks before the last frost. The seed should germinate in a couple of weeks if kept at a temperature of 65 to 70 degrees. Spider flower may be annual, but there is a saying about it: once you have it, you have it. This means that plants reseed and come up plentifully year after year. If you should want to prevent reseeding, simply cut off the seed pods before they mature and turn brown.

In the cool of late afternoon, spider flower pops open with fresh new blooms.

AT A GLANCE

SPIDER FLOWER
Cleome hasslerana

Features: tall, dramatic, heat-tolerant plant

Colors: white, pink, lavender

Height: 3 to 5 feet

Light: full sun to light shade

Soil: well drained

Water: low

Pests: Japanese beetles

Remarks: easy, old-fashioned flower ideal for cottage gardens

This pure white selection is an exception to the typical spider flower, which is usually bicolored.

Different Selections

The common species found in old gardens features bicolored blossoms of lilac and white that fade in the heat. Newer selections come in solid colors and do not fade as quickly. Among them are White Queen, Rose Queen, Cherry Queen, Ruby Queen, Violet Queen, and Helen Campbell, a white selection.

Troubleshooting

Plants tend to grow straight up with few flowering stalks, but you can prevent this by snipping a few inches off the top of each developing stalk before it blooms; two flowering stalks will replace it. Do this two or three times and by midsummer the plant will be smothered in blossoms. Remove the seed pods as they form and the plant will bloom until frost.

Japanese beetles may sometimes eat both the flowers and the foliage. See page 123 for more about Japanese beetles.

Tall, white spider flower—ringed by low-growing petunias—creates a light, cloudlike effect in the midst of summer.

Sunflower

Once relegated to the backyard, sunflowers are now a proud annual in the most prominent beds. Sunflowers have been bred into shorter, more branched plants featuring a variety of broad blooms in yellow, orange, bronze, and even white and bicolored. Their pioneer stock makes them hardy, drought-tolerant plants deservedly popular for borders, as screens, or alone in a showy bed.

Small-flowered, branched selections make excellent cut flowers for a classic, country bouquet or as part of an elegant table setting. Those with a dark *corolla,* the ring around the center of the bloom, make especially lovely cut flowers. For an extra splash of color in the landscape, plant sunflowers with zinnias, another great annual for cutting. The traditional selections, with one giant bloom atop an 8-foot stalk, produce seeds for roasting or for feeding birds. Because of their impressive size, these mammoth types are great fun for children to grow.

Planting and Care

The best way to start sunflowers is to sow seed directly in the garden. Sow in spring after all danger of frost has passed, and choose a spot that gets full sun. Use the spacing recommended on the seed packet, especially for taller plants. If the plants get even a bit of shade from nearby trees in the morning or afternoon, they will grow even taller. Sunflowers do not require much fertilizer but do need water to keep their big leaves from wilting in dry weather; if you do not water,

Sunflower seeds develop at the center of the bloom, turning from green to brown as they mature.

AT A GLANCE

SUNFLOWER
Helianthus annuus

Features: tall summer annual with large blooms

Colors: white, yellow, orange, bronze, bicolored

Height: 15 inches to 10 feet

Light: full sun

Soil: average

Water: low to medium

Pests: none specific

Remarks: easy to grow from seed, great for attracting birds

Small-flowered, branched selections make excellent cut flowers.

Sunflower

Giant sunflowers always bloom facing the sun.

the plants are not likely to die, but the leaves may turn brown on the edges and disfigure a flower bed.

Because mammoth types only produce one big flower, you may wish to stagger plantings a couple of weeks apart to enjoy fresh blooms for a longer time. Even with the smaller-flowered, branching types that produce more blooms as you cut, the initial planting may begin to look bedraggled by the end of summer. Replanting in early summer will give you a fresh crop that lasts through fall. At the end of the season, let the flowers ripen to seed so that you can collect them for next year, or let the seed drop to the ground to come up on its own next spring.

Large sunflowers produce striking flower heads, which can be as large as a dinner plate.

Branched sunflowers, which produce many small blooms, can stand alone in a garden.

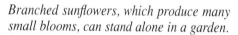

Different Selections

Sunflowers have been hybridized into a variety of ornamental sizes and colors, including plants that branch and produce many flowers. Dwarf selections include Dwarf Sungold, which has double flowers and grows to 15 to 24 inches tall, and Sunspot, which has large 10-inch yellow flowers on plants that stand only 2 feet tall, looking like a shrunken version of a mammoth sunflower.

Medium-height selections are good for flower beds and for cutting. They include Piccolo, which produces 4-foot-tall plants with bright yellow 4-inch flowers; Luna, known for branching plants with lots of pastel yellow blooms on stalks about 5 feet tall; and Italian White, prized for its 4-inch creamy flowers on plants about 4 feet tall. Large-flowered Mixed, which bears 6-inch flowers in yellow, orange, red, and bronze on bushy 5-foot plants, is an attractive selection, for a bed, as is Sunbeam, a 5- to 7-foot plant prized for cutting because of its greenish, pollen-free center.

Among giant selections (8 to 10 feet tall) are Giganteus, Mammoth Russian, and Moonwalker. These are the classic, single-stalked selections that are topped with one giant bloom and used as accents in a garden. The seed of these large selections are the biggest and the best for roasting.

Piccolo is a selection with lemon yellow blooms and a showy dark center. The more you cut it, the more flowers it will produce.

109

Sweet Alyssum

The fine texture of sweet alyssum combines with gerbera for a striking contrast.

Sweet alyssum weaves a carpet of tiny flowers that bring a welcome honey fragrance to the early spring garden. A low-growing, spreading annual, sweet alyssum will grow 6 to 12 inches wide but only 8 inches tall and flourishes in full sun, while the weather is cool.

Because of its creeping growth habit, sweet alyssum makes an excellent choice for containers, edgings, or the front of a border. The plants sometimes flower so exuberantly that they hide their foliage, making a wonderful informal ground cover in a bed of bulbs, such as crocus and hyacinth, or in a rock garden. Plant it in front of sweet William or pansies, or at the base of shrubs. Sweet alyssum is also effective between stones in a pathway or a rock wall, in hanging baskets and window boxes with cascading petunias or pansies, or anywhere you can use a blanket of fragrant flowers.

AT A GLANCE
❖
SWEET ALYSSUM
Lobularia maritima

Features: old-fashioned, fragrant mat of blooms in early spring

Colors: white, lavender, rose, purple

Height: 3 to 8 inches

Light: full sun

Soil: well drained

Water: medium to high

Pests: none specific

Remarks: attractive in pots and window boxes

Planting and Care

You may start sweet alyssum from seed or transplants. Because this is a cool-weather annual, it is important to sow seed in the garden early, four to six weeks before the last frost. Do not cover them; just sprinkle the seed on top of moist soil in full sun or very light shade. The tiny seeds will be easier to spread if you mix them with sand and rake them into the soil very lightly. Transplants set out in early spring can tolerate light frost.

Sweet alyssum begins to bloom five to six weeks after seeding. It will bloom for several months if kept trimmed; otherwise, the blooms will go to seed. Keep the soil moist but do not overwater.

Sweet alyssum enjoys cool, sunny weather. When temperatures rise, sweet alyssum declines. However, if given plenty of water, it will survive in areas with cool summers and will bloom again. You may pull up the old plants and sow new seed in late summer for a fresh second crop in fall. Plants allowed to produce seed will reseed, and seedlings will appear again the following spring.

Different Selections

Popular white selections range from 4 to 6 inches high and include Carpet of Snow, Tiny Tim, and Snow Crystals. Wonderland is a series of 4-inch-tall plants that come in a choice of rose, white, and purple. Violet Queen is prized for its rich violet flowers. Rosie O'Day, an All-America Selections winner, has rosy blooms on 3-inch plants. All selections of sweet alyssum are quite fragrant.

Sow sweet alyssum between paving stones for a sweet-smelling carpet in early spring.

Mix sweet alyssum with petunias in a pot and place in a sunny location.

111

Sweet Pea

Climbing sweet peas are vinelike annuals that need a fence or trellis on which to climb.

AT A GLANCE

❖

SWEET PEA
Lathyrus odoratus

Features: colorful, fragrant
  spring vine or bush
Colors: red, purple, lilac, white,
  pink, blue
Height: 9 inches to 8 feet
Light: full sun to light shade
Soil: moist, fertile, neutral to
  slightly alkaline
Water: medium to high
Pests: aphids, slugs, spider mites
Remarks: does not like hot
  weather

The appeal of this charming annual, which thrives in cool weather, is its fluffy, translucent blooms that spring from slender stems. Sweet peas may be one of many colors—red, deep purple, lilac, white, pale pink, or blue—and always enliven their surroundings with a distinctive honey-orange scent.

There are two forms of sweet peas that may be easily grown from seed. Bush or dwarf types, which grow about 2½ feet tall, are good for beds, borders, and containers. Plant these sweet peas near spring bulbs so that they may hide the fading foliage of bulbs. Climbing types, which can grow up to 8 feet in length, make charming accent vines and screens. These will easily climb fences, gateposts, and other vertical structures. Both types provide delightful blooms for cutting to bring indoors.

Planting and Care

Sow sweet pea seeds in the fall in the Lower and Coastal South. Sow in early spring in cooler climates, as soon as the ground can be worked. Good timing is essential, as sweet pea does not like hot weather and needs to be established and blooming before summer's heat begins. In areas where you can plant in fall, it will overwinter, even if the tops of the plants appear to die. Growth resumes vigorously from the roots in spring. You may also start sweet peas indoors six weeks before transplanting outdoors.

Sweet pea likes full sun to light shade and rich, moist soil. If your soil is acid, bring the pH up to 7 by adding lime. Prepare a rich bed by digging a trench a foot deep and equally wide; fill it with organic matter before sowing seed.

Soak the large seeds for several hours before planting. They will absorb water faster if you nick the surface with a nail file. Plant seeds 6 inches apart, poking them about ½ inch into the soil. When seedlings appear, mulch them to keep the roots cool. Water regularly and deadhead old blooms to ensure that the plant continues to flower until the weather gets hot.

Both types of sweet pea have very thin stems that need support. Plants grab their supports with thin, curly tendrils, like those of edible peas. Always use thin twig, wire, or string supports, because the tendrils cannot wrap around thick props. Climbing types may be staked with a bean trellis, chicken wire, bamboo canes or twigs arranged in a tepee, or a wire fence. Dwarf selections do not need much support; simply prop them up with twigs.

Different Selections

Many gardeners prefer older selections that are quite heat tolerant, like the first wild sweet pea believed to have originated in Italy. Pink Perfume, a 15-inch bush type, produces pale pink flowers and a pleasing fragrance. Also available in an array of colors are Patio Mixed, an early-blooming 9-inch bush and Bijou, an early-blooming 10- to 12-inch bush. Any of these would work well in a window box or a pot, or as an edging plant.

Supersnoop, which grows to about 2½ feet tall, blooms early, making it a good choice for places where spring warms up quickly. Old Spice is a collection of old-fashioned, fragrant climbing selections from Sicily; Royal Family Mixed is a fine climbing sweet pea, with large flowers and some resistance to heat. Galaxy Mixed is another climber that boasts long, strong stems with five or more large flowers.

Troubleshooting

Sweet peas are frequently bothered by aphids, slugs, and spider mites. Turn to pages 122 and 124 for more about these pests.

The butterfly-like blossoms of sweet peas are so named for their sweet fragrance.

Sweet William

This dwarf selection of mixed colors stays very compact, making it an ideal choice for the edge of a garden.

Sweet William has been a fragrant part of American gardens since colonial days. When planted liberally, its light scent in early spring perfumes the garden and invites butterflies, and its blooms are a delightful addition to an arrangement of cut flowers.

Often planted in fall to bloom the next spring, sweet William is a dependable and showy annual for the cool months of spring. Its large clusters of fragrant flowers also make sweet William a nice choice for pots near the terrace or deck. Indoors, one cut stem practically makes a whole bouquet of pinks, as they are often called.

Planting and Care

Sweet William may behave like a biennial. If planted in the spring, it will grow throughout the summer to become a thick clump of foliage, about 18 inches across. The plentiful leaves help keep the garden green through winter. In the mild winters of the South, the foliage will withstand freezing. It may droop overnight during extreme cold, but it will perk up as the day warms. (Although biennial, some selections have been so improved by breeding that they will bloom the first spring if planted early.)

Plants may be started from seed or transplants. Plant in rich, organic soil in full sun (with afternoon shade) and good drainage. If your garden has acid soil, sprinkle 1 cup of lime for every 10 square feet before planting. In the South, set out transplants or sow seed directly in the garden in fall for spring color; farther north, sow in early spring

Flowers of sweet William are clustered into showy balls that brighten a spring border.

for summer flowers. Sweet William will often reseed itself, providing year after year of fragrant blossoms. You can also collect seeds or dig young seedlings to transplant in the spring.

Cutting spent flowers before they produce seed will keep plants blooming longer, but the flowers must remain on the plant in order to reseed.

Different Selections

Sweet William has changed very little over time. It blooms in white, purples, and pinks to crimson, the same as it has for years. There are also dwarf types available.

Selections include Pride of Park Avenue, with graceful, 18- to 24-inch stems that carry brightly colored blooms and are tall enough to stand in a vase. Indian Carpet is a dwarf selection that grows into a ruglike ground cover of 8-inch tall flowering stalks. Wee Willie is even more compact (3 to 6 inches) and is good for edging, with single blooms available in a mixture of colors.

Sweet William will perfume an entire garden in spring.

Wax Begonia

The glossy green leaves of Victory White wax begonias make the blossoms appear even whiter.

Cool and crisp on even the hottest of days, wax begonia creates a steady show of color from early spring until frost. The offspring of plants native to Brazil, today's hybrids boast upturned, succulent green or bronze leaves and ground-hugging clouds of small silky flowers. The blooms, in elegant reds, creamy whites, and sedate pinks, add reliable color to any area of your garden. In rain or shine, sun or shade, begonias work well in flower beds and borders, as well as window boxes and other containers.

Wax begonias are most attractive in the garden when planted in gently curving lines. Ranging from 6 to 12 inches tall, they also make excellent edging plants for walkways and the borders of raised beds. Small groupings of three to five plants can serve as spots of color in a shaded or partially sunny border. Wax begonias are also naturals for pots and window boxes because they are heat-hardy and their delicate flowers can be best appreciated when viewed up close. Combine green-leafed selections with ferns, coleus, or caladiums for a refreshing niche in the shade. Bronze-leafed selections make comely companions for silver plants, such as annual dusty miller or perennial artemisia.

Planting and Care

Set out transplants after all danger of frost has passed. Plant in rich soil that retains moisture but drains well. If you have poor drainage, amend the soil with compost and other organic material, or add extra soil to raise the beds. Wax begonias do well under hot, humid conditions, although they may bloom less profusely during the sultry days of August. Then, you will appreciate the color and texture of their leaves as much as their blooms.

Wax begonias are drought tolerant once established, but do not let new transplants dry out. In the absence of rain, water once a week. However, be careful with container plants; their roots are likely to rot, so do not overwater. Allow the top layer, about 1 inch of soil, to dry between waterings. If container plants start to look leggy in late summer, pinch dead flowers and unwieldy sprouts.

Wax begonias will need extra fertilizer in midsummer; apply a slow-release flower food. (See page 28 to read about fertilizers.) If your begonias look tired by September, consider replacing them with a new set of transplants, which will be in the garden centers for fall.

Wax begonias make excellent edging plants, providing a tidy contrast to the surrounding landscape.

Different Selections

Green-leafed selections are well suited for shade, while the bronze-leafed selections take more sun. For partial or morning sun locations, the best series is the bronze-leafed Cocktail Series, which grows from 6 to 8 inches tall. Selections include Gin, with deep pink flowers, Vodka, with red flowers, Brandy, with light pink flowers, and Whiskey, with white flowers.

Among green-leafed wax begonias is the tried-and-true Olympia series, which includes blooms in white, pink, red, salmon, and starlet (white with rosy red margins). The Encore series includes both bronze- and green-leafed selections, such as the lovely Encore White/Bronze, with dramatic dark leaves. Encore begonias grow about a foot tall and are a bit more floppy that other selections, resulting in a looser appearance than the more tightly mounded types.

Wax begonias can handle the occasional dry conditions of a container; their mounding habit is perfect for bowls.

Zinnia

With flowers held high on sturdy stems, tall zinnias are prized for both flower beds and cutting gardens.

Zinnias are hard to beat for spectacular color and dependable blooms from summer through fall. Their brilliant color makes them a yearly favorite for the seasoned gardener, and their ease and dependability make them perfect for the inexperienced, too. Zinnias are ideal cut flowers, as no other annual offers as many colorful blooms for cutting. The cut flowers last about a week and do not shed their leaves when they die; they simply fade and then turn brown.

Zinnias come in a full range of plant heights and flower sizes suited for either flower beds or cutting gardens. You can plant them in a solid mass of one color, set out a few plants as summer filler in a perennial border, use low plants for edging and containers, or mix all the colors together in a bed or border for a fiesta of flowers. They are also excellent plants for a child's garden because they do well in summer, sprout quickly, attract butterflies, and bloom in so many bright colors.

Planting and Care

You may start zinnias from seed or from purchased transplants. The seeds are large and easy to sow; plant at least two weeks after the last frost. In the South, you can sow zinnias as late as July for color in late summer and early fall. Choose a sunny location with well-drained soil. Zinnias are not fussy about soil but will bloom best in rich, moist ground, such as that of a vegetable garden. In fact, vegetable gardeners will sometimes plant a row of zinnias in the garden to attract bees for pollination. Water zinnias regularly until they are established; although forgiving in dry weather, they will bloom more and the foliage will be healthier if if they are well watered during periods of drought. Keep zinnias blooming furiously by fertilizing every six weeks with a slow-release flower food and by cutting spent blooms so that the plants will produce more.

The more you cut zinnias, the more they bloom. Otherwise, they will go to seed, stop blooming, and die. If you want long, unbranched stems for cutting, remove side branches as the plant grows. This technique will also give you the largest flowers. Plants growing 24 inches and taller should be staked, especially in areas prone to summer thunderstorms.

Different Selections

Zinnias come in two flower shapes. Those with flat-petaled blooms are known as dahlia flowered and have a perfect geometric fullness. They include the California Giants and Giant Sun Hybrids, an All-America Selections winner. Cactus-flowered zinnias have petals which curl along the sides, giving the blossom a feathery, irregular outline. Among these are All-America Selections winners Wild Cherry, Carved Ivory, and the more mildew-resistant Zenith Hybrids; also available are Rosy Future, Torch, Firecracker, and Yellow Zenith.

Zinnia plants come in four sizes, lending them to many uses in the garden. Extra dwarf plants bloom the earliest and include the Thumbelina and Mini series. Plants are about 6 inches tall with mounded form, good for borders and containers. Dwarfs grow from 7 to 14 inches tall. This group includes the Pinwheel series, which have small single flowers and creep like a ground cover rather than growing upright like other selections. Other dwarfs, such as the Peter Pan series, an All-America Selections winner, have large flowers atop small plants and appear to be shrunken versions of taller types. They may be used for colorful impact at the front of a border, for mass plantings, and in containers.

Zinnias offer long-lasting cut flowers in an assortment of brilliant colors.

Narrowleaf zinnia creeps like a ground cover, softening a walkway with mounds of flowers.

The half-tall category includes the Lilliput series and the mildew-resistant Sun series; both grow from 18 to 24 inches tall and are popular for cutting. Tall ones reach a height of 24 to 36 inches. These include the Ruffles Hybrids, known for ruffled double blooms that are 2 to 4 inches wide and are popular for borders and cottage gardens as well as for cutting. The Zenith hybrids have blooms up to 6 inches wide and are spectacular for cutting.

Dahlia-flowered zinnias have flat petals and are perfectly symmetrical in form.

The curved petals of this cactus-flowered zinnia give the bloom a ruffled look.

AT A GLANCE

❖
NARROWLEAF ZINNIA
Zinnia angustifolia

Features: very heat tolerant; nonstop blooms until frost

Colors: orange, creamy white

Height: 12 inches

Light: full sun

Soil: well drained

Water: low to medium

Pests: powdery mildew

Remarks: looks like a wildflower

Narrowleaf Zinnia

Narrowleaf zinnia *(Zinnia angustifolia)*, which is a different species from the standard garden zinnia, has the look of a wildflower. A dependable, heat-tolerant annual, it blooms from spring until frost and is covered with daisylike flowers in orange or white. It grows into a multibranched, creeping plant about 12 inches tall and twice as wide with slender, blue-green leaves. Because of its growth habit, this zinnia is popular for massing like a ground cover or planting where it can spill over a wall or the edge of a container. Its loose, wildflower-like habit also makes narrowleaf zinnia suitable for sunny areas of a natural, informal landscape. You may sometimes see it sold as *Zinnia linearis,* its former scientific name.

Narrowleaf zinnia may also be started from seed or from transplants and needs the same conditions and care as other zinnias.

Troubleshooting

In humid climates, zinnias are prone to powdery mildew, a fungus that looks like white mildew on the foliage and will cause the leaves to wither. Avoid watering with overhead sprinklers; use a soaker hose instead and water in early morning so plants have time to dry. Adequate spacing between plants will also provide good air circulation so that the leaves can dry quickly after a rain. The best way to avoid powdery mildew is to plant mildew-resistant selections, such as the Zenith hybrids. Turn to page 123 to read more about powdery mildew.

Be prepared to support tall zinnias with thin stakes or grow-through plant supports. Their flowers are often so big and heavy that even the sturdiest stems are bent by rain.

Pink and yellow zinnias are the focal point of this summer bed at Callaway Gardens in Pine Mountain, Georgia.

Pests and Diseases

The following insects and diseases are common pests of the annuals in this book. To control them, you must first know your enemy; learn which plants are susceptible, what symptoms may occur, and how to combat the pests. Turn to page 125 for tips on the proper handling and usage of pesticides. For more information about specific pesticides, contact your local Extension office, which is listed under the county Department of Agriculture in your blue pages.

Aphids

Aphids

Aphids are tiny, pear-shaped insects about ⅛ to ¼ inch long; they are frequently green or black but may also be yellow or pink. They harm plants by sucking sap from the tender young stems and flower buds so that growth is distorted and the buds do not open. Aphids are usually worst in spring and fall. They will produce hundreds of offspring in a few weeks, so it is crucial to control them as soon as they appear.

Cabbageworms and Other Caterpillars

Cabbageworms are green, velvety caterpillars that chew holes in leaves. They are primarily pests of the vegetable garden but will attack ornamental cabbage and kale, which are relatives of the culinary types. Control these caterpillars as soon as you can because their feeding will disfigure the leaves. They hide on the underside of the leaves and in the crown of the plant; spray or dust these areas very carefully.

Other caterpillars may attack the leaves and buds of annuals, especially those with large, succulent leaves. To control these pests, be sure to spray the underside of the leaves thoroughly and keep a caterpillar dust on the foliage to prevent reinfestation.

Hollyhock Rust

This disease can destroy an entire planting of hollyhocks. Signs of the disease are yellow areas on the surface of the leaves and orange, rustlike spots on the underside. You may also see long, dark lesions on the stalks. The best way to control rust is to purchase selections that are rust resistant. Remove old plants from the garden once they have faded; if left untended, they provide a source for infection the following year. For plants that are already infected, spray both sides of the leaves and the stems with a recommended fungicide.

Japanese Beetles

These ½-inch-long, metallic green-and-copper beetles will fly into your garden and are very difficult to control. They feed on many plants but are especially fond of hollyhocks. Japanese beetles like to chew one plant for a short time and then fly to another plant. They usually feed in hordes, with hundreds present at a time.

Dusting foliage with a recommended pesticide helps, but you must keep the dust on new growth as it unfurls. The best way to control Japanese beetles is to kill the *grubs,* or larvae, which feed in the lawn. To do this most effectively, join forces with neighbors, who are doubtless being affected by this pest as well, to treat a large area.

Nematodes

Nematodes are soil-borne microscopic creatures that attack the roots of many plants. Their feeding prevents the roots from functioning properly, so plants are stunted and may die. Unfortunately, there is no simple solution to nematodes. Strategies include removing the soil, switching to less susceptible plants, and maintaining the overall health of the plants in your garden. Contact your Extension office for more information.

Japanese beetle

Powdery Mildew

Powdery mildew is a disease that looks like a white to gray mildew on the surface of the leaves. It will cause the leaves to dry and wither, thus weakening the plant. To control powdery mildew, be sure that plants are not crowded; good air circulation is important to keep the foliage dry so that powdery mildew will not develop.

Once the disease appears, it is difficult to control. Therefore, you should spray both sides of the leaves with an approved fungicide before the mildew appears. If you have seen the disease in your garden before, you can generally predict its occurrence (usually in spring and fall).

Powdery mildew is likely to affect zinnias and celosia. To avoid the problem, look for selections that have been bred with resistance to the disease.

Powdery mildew

Slug

Slugs

Slugs are like snails without shells. They chew holes in the succulent leaves of young plants. Slugs feed at night, so you will not see them unless you turn over a rock or a handful of mulch to find where they hide during the day. One sure sign of slugs is a shiny slime trail on the leaves in your garden. To see the trail clearly, hold an affected leaf in the sunlight and turn it so that the light is reflected by the slimy trail.

You can control slugs with bait, but read the label warning carefully, as most are poisonous to pets. You may trap slugs in shallow bowls of beer or beneath cantaloupe or grapefruit halves turned upside down in the garden. If you have a pond or water garden you may bring in toads, which will eat slugs.

Spider Mites

Spider mites are tiny spiderlike insects that collect on the underside of the leaves and on flower buds. They damage plants by sucking sap from the plants so that the leaves are deformed and the buds do not open. They are worst in spring and fall, especially during dry weather. You may not see the spider mites until their feeding begins to make the topside of the leaves look faded and mottled. Turning a leaf over will reveal clusters of pinpoint-sized spider mites and often their delicate webbing. Use a magnifying glass to be sure.

To control spider mites, spray the underside of the leaves thoroughly. Spider mites love lantana, hollyhock, rose verbena, and sweet pea, so look for them on these plants in particular.

Spider mite damage

Whiteflies

These white, mothlike insects are only ⅛ inch long and can usually be seen on the underside of young leaves. If you shake the plant, they will fly out and then light again. They suck sap from the leaves, leaving foliage yellowed and spotted. Ageratum, lantana, geranium, and rose verbena are favorites of this pest. To control whiteflies, spray the underside of the leaves with a recommended pesticide.

Pesticides

Many techniques and pesticides are available to help you fight diseases and insect pests, but the recommendations for using these products frequently change. Contact your local Extension office for information about specific pesticides.

Before using a pesticide, read the entire label. Always use pesticides strictly according to label directions. Using a pesticide in any way that is not in accordance with label recommendations is illegal.

Tips for Using Pesticides

• Try milder pesticides, such as insecticidal soap, before using stronger substances.

• Use only the amount directed at the time and under the conditions specified.

• Use sprays or dusts on a still, windless day.

• Never transfer pesticides from their containers.

• Keep a set of measuring spoons on a key ring; store by slipping the ring over the wand of your sprayer.

• Always store pesticides in a cool, dry place. Extreme heat or freezing weather may reduce the effectiveness of some products.

• When spraying foliage, be sure to cover the underside of the leaves, and do not forget the stems. Spraying just the top of the leaves will not control spider mites and other insects that live on the underside of the leaves.

• Adjust your nozzle to deliver a fine mist; tiny droplets will adhere to foliage better than a coarse spray.

HOW PESTICIDES ARE PACKAGED

Solutions are bottled concentrates that need to be mixed with water. In some cases, they are already diluted and are ready for use.

Aerosols contain a solvent in an aerosol spray that is ready for immediate use.

Dusts contain a very fine, dry carrier, such as talc. They are ready to use and are applied dry.

Granular pesticides, which are usually used on lawns, are similar to dusts but contain larger and heavier particles.

Baits contain food or other ingredients to attract the pest. Slug control is often a bait.

Wettable powders are dry, finely ground formulations that are generally mixed with water for spray application. The key to their use is to keep the mixture agitated so that the powder does not settle to the bottom of the sprayer.

Index

Special Thanks

Ball Seed Company

David Durham, photograph, 68

Jennifer Greer

Goldsmith Seeds, Inc.

PanAmerican Seed Company

Southern Progress Corporation
Library Staff